Did Beatniks Kill John F. Kennedy?

Bongo Joe's Requiem for the President

By Rob Johnson

Published by Beatdom Books

Published by Beatdom Books

Copyright © 2018 by Rob Johnson
Cover © Reynaldo Alvardo, Jr.

All rights reserved. No part of this book may be reproduced in any form or by any electronic or mechanical means including information storage and retrieval systems, without permission in writing from the author. The only exception is by a reviewer, who may quote short excerpts in a review.

View the publisher's website:
www.books.beatdom.com

Printed in the United Kingdom

First Print Edition
ISBN 978-0-9934099-2-9

Portions of this book are adapted from an essay published in Volume 2 of the *Journal of Beat Studies* (2013), "Did Beatniks Kill John F. Kennedy?" Used by permission.
"Bongo Joe" appears in *This River Here: Poems of San Antonio* (San Antonio: Wings Press, 2014) by Carmen Tafolla. Quoted with permission.

Did Beatniks Kill John F. Kennedy?

George Coleman, a.k.a. "Calypso Joe," pushes a wheelbarrow to a stop on Galveston's Seawall in front of the Pleasure Pier, an amusement park built over the Gulf of Mexico. It's a summer day in 1957 and the Seawall is crowded with holiday tourists. Calliope music, the roar of the Mountain Speedway roller coaster, and the noises of cars cruising Seawall Blvd. float out over the Gulf. Sea-washed blocks of pink granite, placed at the concave base of the 17-foot-high Seawall to prevent erosion, glint in the sun. The Seawall is the longest sidewalk in the world, at 10.3 miles, but in Eisenhower's very orderly America Joe is the only street performer on its entire length, the only man who sees no reason why that lovely long wide sidewalk can't be a public stage.

Joe pushes his brightly-painted wheelbarrow to the edge of the sidewalk fronting the pier and adjusts his cargo—six large cans he's bought for fifty cents from a junkyard, painted green and mounted on the wheelbarrow. Tourists are already eyeing him with a mixture of caution and interest. He stands over six feet, a physically powerful, deeply black-skinned Negro dressed in a ragged t-shirt, cut-off shorts, and sandals split at the toe: he looks as if he has just washed up on the Galveston shore, the lone survivor of a shipwreck. He begins by tuning the "drums" with a crowbar, bending the metal rims and occasionally knocking a hole in the side of the can.

When a few curious tourists gather around, Joe begins finding a beat, concentrating deeply, taking his cue from the rhythm of the waves or the clattering of the wooden rollercoaster warping in the perpetual gulf humidity, then shifts into one of his numbers, a version of the gospel song, "This Old World is in a Terrible Condition." He's part preacher, clown, philosopher, and con man, playing the dozens while stroking his drums with sticks he's attached a child's rattle to, doubling the rhythm. Drivers on the Seawall occasionally honk their horns, adding to the music.

Yeah, sisters and brothers, he begins loudly in a high-pitched voice that sounds like raspy laughter.

> *I really hate to say*
> *That our world is in a terrible condition*
> *If you want to go to heaven when you D-I-E*
> *Check your heart where you please*
> *And bring your money to me*

He nods at his "kitty," a box with a few coins in the bottom. The song is a standard Negro spiritual, sometimes sung as a Jeremiad to bring back the flock, but George turns it into a send-up of religious hypocrisy set right there in Galveston:

> *I gotta gal*
> *She's alright*
> *She lives on Post Office Street*
> *And all my beloved church friends turned me down*

Rob Johnson

*Hadn't been for her I wouldn't have had a bite to eat
I declare, this old world is in a terrible condition*

He drums without words for a spell and changes tack, letting the rhythm help him develop his theme. He makes the old spiritual topical, playing on the "space race" and the Cold War he's been reading about in popular science magazines and *Time* in the cool of the Rosenberg public library.

*Off I go into Arctic
Seeking for Mars
The most beautiful of all the stars
When you hear a peculiar noise
Don't be scared, it'll be me
Off to orbit
A-men
Cause this old world, the planet earth
Is in a terrible condition*

He signs off at the end of the lengthy, improvised number:

*Tune in every night
Same station
Get to hear Father G. O. Dough Coleman
65000 on your dial
This is station WBUL Galveston*

Joe laughs maniacally, barks, and spits like a cat—and makes one more plea for some money.

*Sisters and brothers
The only difference between me and your Baptist preacher
He's inside and I'm out of doors
He knows the basic principles and ethics
But I know the score*

Did Beatniks Kill John F. Kennedy?

The only difference between his dollar and my dollar
Is the serial number
Can ya all say 'dat'?
How to do
Who to do
And out
That was your Reverend.

After the number, Joe lets a small child hit on his drums as the kitty rattles a few donations. If he's a success, he can make as much as ten dollars on a weekend day.

Later that afternoon, he sees three skinny white teenagers, rock and rollers, walking towards him intent on causing trouble, or at least he can see such thoughts in their eyes. He keeps playing the rhythms on his metal drums. The teenagers stop and form a semi-circle around Joe and his drums and he can see them softening their aggressive stance: they start to listen to the music in spite of themselves, their Chucks keeping the beat. After a while they turn away and head down the Seawall. One teen guiltily hangs back and tosses some money at Joe.

That night, June, 1957, Joe plays well into the evening. His last listener of the night is a policeman, Officer C. W. Henson. "Joe," the officer tells him matter-of-factly, "There's been some complaints about the noise you're making. You're going have to come with me. Disturbing the peace." Joe stands his ground politely. "Officer, I always held my place with anybody and do my best not to offend. Ask anyone around here. You can't hear my music half a block away over the music coming from this pier," Joe says, gesturing to the starry colored lights and racket of the carnival behind him. But Officer Henson's not listening, or can't.

Officer Henson books Joe for disturbing the peace at 10 pm Sunday night. Monday morning, a judge sets the fine at twenty-five dollars, but Joe only has two dollars to give. It's money Joe needs for his rent on R1/2 street in the Negro section of Galveston, so he elects to work off the fine with an 8-day jail stay.

In Texas in the 1950s, a black man learns to be philosophical.

A few days into his jail stay, a reporter from *The Galveston Daily News* stops by, having heard there is an interesting character behind bars. Fred Wortham sees and makes note of Joe's brightly colored wheelbarrow and drums stashed in the corner of the drab jail.

"Calypso Joe," Wortham begins. Joe has lifted his name from a movie of the same title, currently playing a nearby drive-in. In the movie, Calypso Joe's band helps a young TV producer woo his white girlfriend back from the arms of a swarthy South American millionaire, alleviating the audience's fear of miscegenation. "Why'd they bring you in, Calypso?"

"They said I was disturbing the peace, but the thing I can't quite understand is who made the complaints against me and why." He is genuinely puzzled and let down by the human race, not the first nor last time. "I always stopped before the Pleasure Pier music stops every night. It's disappointing. But the Lord knows what he's doing, so I'll have to take it as it comes."

Wortham can tell he has an interesting interview on his hands and settles in a chair inside Joe's cell to listen. "What's your real name, Calypso Joe, if you don't mind stating it for the record. And how did you pick the pier for your 'concert hall'?"

Joe tells him his story.

George "Calypso Joe" Coleman is born on November 28, 1923 in Haines City, Florida, near Orlando. The Coleman family roots, though, are in the Bahamas, islands Joe sometimes wistfully sings about in his improvised songs. His father dies before he is born, and his mother, a churchgoing woman who teaches him a little piano, passes when he is seven. For a time, he and his sister live in a Florida orphanage. There's a piano in the orphanage, and Joe teaches himself music—he never learns to read it—by first playing the black keys. He's a natural-born musical talent and multi-instrumentalist: saxophone, clarinet, percussion, any musical instrument he can get hold of. He leaves the orphanage at the age of 14, odd-jobbing his way across Depression-era America, and eventually rejoins his sister, who has moved to Detroit. Detroit in the early 1940s has a thriving jazz, blues, and vaudeville scene, and 18-year-old Joe's musical talent lands him in a number of bands playing whatever is needed—drums, piano, horns. He develops a sophisticated ear, appreciating the big band music of the times as well as the revolutionary hot jazz, bebop jazz. Jazz makes its mark on Joe and is reflected in his spontaneous compositions and the off-key chords he whistles during his Seawall performances.

In Detroit, in 1941, he gigs as a backup musician for the Will Mastin Trio, featuring phenomenon Sammy Davis, Jr. Davis, who has been singing and dancing since the age of 3, is a soft shoe master in tux and tails, and performs in the vaudeville act with his father and uncle. He has toured the United States twenty-three times by 1941, when Joe meets him and they become friends. That year, at Detroit's Michigan Theater, Davis also meets Frank Sinatra for the first time when the Will Mastin Trio fills in for "Tip Tap Toe," the opening act for The Tommy Dorsey Band. Sinatra, whose talent as Dorsey's singer is already overshadowing Dorsey himself, is wowed by sixteen-year-old Davis' performance and finds him backstage: "I'm Frank Sinatra." After the War, Sinatra goes out of his way to hire the Will Mastin Trio for lucrative opening act bills at the Capitol Theater in New York. They make four times their weekly salary in one night. Sinatra himself introduces the Mastin Trio and publicly embraces Sammy Davis, Jr. on stage—an almost unheard of gesture in 1946 by a white performer.

In later years, according to a close friend of Joe's, he is called on by Sammy and his crowd to play late-night, after-hours parties when they are performing in Texas cities. Joe plays blues piano brilliantly and shares a sense of the past with these men.

During World War II, both Joe and Sammy entertain troops as part of the Entertainment Corps (Sammy enters the Army in 1942, Joe in 1943). Davis has largely been sheltered from racism in America and is shocked by the treatment he receives from white soldiers. He fights back mainly, he says, the only way he knows how: "My talent was the weapon, the power, the way for me to fight. It was the one way I might hope to affect a man's thinking." Joe performs stateside in Officer's Clubs and PXs, driving a truck by day. The musical equipment is top-notch and in later years he often dreams of being able to play the service-issue drums again. "Man, I could go on those hides," he tells the *Daily News* reporter. A picture from those years shows him tap-dancing dressed in top hat and tails with a cane, performing routines he learned on the vaudeville circuit.

At the end of the war, in 1946, he separates from the military in Fort Sheridan, Illinois, spends some time on the road in Oklahoma, and in 1949 lands for a short period of time in Beaumont, Texas, a petrochemical town near the large southern city of Houston. Soon, Joe finds his way to Houston.

Thousands of blacks along the gulf coast come to Houston after the war hoping for work in the oil industry, and by mid-century Houston has one of the largest populations of blacks in any Southern city. They bring with them unique musical talents. Street musicians gather downtown in front of Jackson's Shoe Repair Shine Parlor at Milam and Prairie, where cab drivers get a shine and downtowners pause for the entertainment. Joe finds his way into this downtown sidewalk symphony. "Just trying to get a job as a drummer, and I couldn't get the job unless I had my own drums," he explains to the reporter from his jail cell in 1957. "I tried to make a loan from several sources and couldn't get the money. So I got some cans and fixed them up like drums and started playing on street corners in Houston." He's a multi-instrumentalist but says, "I always did like the rhythmic-type music, such as xylophone, piano, drum. Anything you bang on, that's what I always liked." To Joe, a piano is the same as a drum—you bang on it.

He first plays the Seawall in Galveston, about thirty miles south of Houston, in the summer of 1954. On weekends during the summer months, the Texas Gulfliner passenger train runs every half hour until midnight from downtown Houston to Galveston beach and back, twenty-five cents for a round-trip ticket. Joe sits in the black's only passenger section: you can tell which section you are in by the thickness of the seat cushions. The Gulfliner crosses Galveston Bay on a brave bridge lapped by the green sea chop and Joe disembarks on Galveston Island at the Atcheson, Topeka, and Santa Fe Depot, with its vaulted ceilings, marble columns, and mahogany benches. Joe is penniless in this splendid setting, taking it all in as crowds of tourists part around him, but he walks happily outside the station through a grove of oleanders, past the Henderson House restaurant, and onto 25th Street. He follows the sound of the surf to the Gulf and sets foot on the Seawall for the first time: it's the same gulf breeze of Florida he breathes in familiarly, and he's never seen such an inviting long sidewalk stage. Soon he's scavenged some cans and brings his Houston street-corner routine to the Seawall. When he's arrested in 1957 for disturbing the peace he is living behind Menard Park in a boarding house owned by a prominent black businessman, Gus Allen. It's only three blocks from the Seawall and The Pleasure Pier.

The showplace of the Gulf Coast sits on The Pleasure Pier, the Balinese Room, a nightclub and gambling parlor built by mobster Sam Maceo, who controls vice in Galveston for decades. Frank Sinatra plays there in 1950. No longer a teen idol and now suffering through a divorce from Nancy Sinatra, Sinatra can only find work in mob-controlled casinos. He's known Maceo since the late 1940s when Maceo visited his Palm Springs home. Maceo pays him a standard singer's fee to perform at the Balinese and Frank slums it at the Towers Motel and eats chili and beans at the Speedway Café, next to The Pleasure Pier's rollercoaster.

Joe never plays joints like the Balinese.

"Wouldn't you rather be playing in a nightclub then, rather than on the Seawall, Joe?" Wortham asks him, somewhat skeptically.

"No, I was looking for a place where there was a good clean atmosphere and where the people who wanted to listen to me could, regardless of their likes and dislikes insofar as a nightclub or other type of business house. I guess I could make more money in a nightclub or something, but this way those who want to hear me can and I like the beach very much. Through the 'kitty' made up by the listeners every night, the Good Lord has seen I've got a place to stay and food in my stomach."

What he doesn't tell the reporter is that his choice of career as a street performer also keeps him out of the control of mobsters, like Sam Maceo, and helps him avoid the humiliation of playing segregated southern nightclubs and concert halls. Even Sammy Davis, Jr. can't get a room in the Vegas hotels where he performs until Sinatra appeals to his mob bosses in 1960.

The county jailer, George Lundy, has been listening in on the interview and interrupts Wortham to verify some of Joe's claims: "Fred, I tell you what, I used to promote some acts over in La Porte, and I seen this man, and he's a one-man band and a first-class entertainer."

They are both looking at Joe, appraisingly.

"Where are you going to go when you get out, Joe?" Wortham asks.

Joe shrugs. "As long as there are open-minded folks who want to listen to my parables on truth and honesty and want to hear my music, call it calypso or bongo or whatever, I'll make out fine and be happy. Unless there is something real wrong, me and the drums will go back out to the Seawall for a while."

Did Beatniks Kill John F. Kennedy?

"From Wail to Jail" runs in the *The Galveston Daily News* on the 21st of August, 1957. On Wednesday morning, a Galveston promoter named Jack Sayre reads the story about Joe's inconveniences and pays the remaining twenty-three dollars of his fine. Sayre owns property on Stewart Beach and invites Joe to play there, safe from police harassment. "I can't help it, but I will always help the little man who is down. Coleman can set up here on the property and play as long as he wants to," he says.

Fresh out of jail and back on the beach, Coleman breathes in the free gulf breeze and says in a follow-up story in the *News*, "This is where a man belongs. Where it's clean, cool and wholesome. I'm indebted to Mr. Sayre and all the other friends who've helped me and the drums will prove it." Claude Allen, operator of the Pleasure Pier's Golden Garter Tavern, also offers to help out Joe. Two people had complained about Joe according to police. They will not identify the callers.

The following night, Joe plays conga drums at the Blue Room Teen Club. He never fails to make a lasting impression on his young listeners in Galveston. Houston-raised record producer, Billy Bentley, says decades later that the first concert he ever saw was Calypso Joe on the Seawall in 1957. Joe impresses him as much as seeing Elvis on the Ed Sullivan Show.

After Labor Day, the kids head back to school and the Seawall empties of tourists. A stray norther makes it down to Galveston in October and the Gulf turns grey and choppy. In the fall and winter months Joe sets up shop again on the streets of downtown Houston. Necessity and Houston's petrochemical industry now hand him the instrument that will shape his signature sound: from small cans he finds in alleyways he moves to the big kettle-sized 55-gallon oil drums with their chined sides made for easy rolling. These he scavenges in the warehouse district bordering downtown. He cuts the barrels, bends them, and pokes holes in them to modify their tone.

Joe's part of a cast of big city characters in downtown Houston—a man with a full Santa Claus beard who sells newspapers on the street corner that December, a trash scavenger who drives a truck with a sign that mysteriously reads, "Blood and Evil Your Judgment." Joe finds a bicycle, paints it fire-engine red and rigs an umbrella on it for shelter and a rack for his drums—two 55-gallon Texaco Superchiefs. This outfit he pedals on the crowded city sidewalks.

People stare at him in his ragged clothes, but he's always smiling and enjoys the attention. Occasionally he sets up his drums outside Pete's shine parlor or on another downtown street corner and starts drumming and whistling. Houston folk-music enthusiast Mack McCormick tracks down Joe's rhythms in the fall or winter of 1957. He's fascinated by Joe and awkwardly tries to strike up a conversation, as Houston blacks and whites live in separate worlds. But Joe sets him at ease and tells him, "If you think I was ever a Negro it is only because you are colorblind and do not see my true color." When communication fails, he says, "Drums are a universal language—I can speak to anyone living or dead." Talking with Joe, McCormick senses an ambivalence about him that is at odds with his need to perform, a kind of double-consciousness all too common in southern blacks who live in the still-segregated South: "He is in suspicious retreat from the society around him and his response to the world is anonymity mingled with exhibitionism," he later writes. McCormick meets Joe again in Galveston, on the Seawall in front of the Murdochs Pier, and records Joe on a battery-operated EMI recorder performing "Gene Krupa's Disc Jockey Jump."

Another of Joe's original improvised monologues from that time period is titled "George Coleman for President, Nobody for Vice-President." It's 1957, almost 1958, and two-term president, Eisenhower, can't run again, leaving the political season open. A young Massachusetts senator named John F. Kennedy is running for re-election to the Senate but he already has his eye on the Democratic presidential nomination in the 1960 election.

1957 marks a tense, science-fiction moment in the Cold War. In early 1957, the Soviet Union successfully tests an intercontinental ballistic missile, and by that fall a Russian satellite, Sputnik, circles the globe, a clearly visible bright light in the night sky that is an insult to America's Emersonian exceptionalism.

It's also the moment most Americans first learn of a subterranean youth culture labelled "Beat" by author Jack Kerouac, whose *On the Road* is released in September. The original Beats are a self-named non-political bunch of post-WWII poets and writers who have studied at Harvard and Columbia but who take their inspiration from Times Square and its habitués—junkies, small-time thieves, prostitutes, homosexuals, negro jazz musicians and other fringe elements ignored by buttoned-up post-war prosperous America. The heretofore obscure Beat movement becomes known nationwide when Allen Ginsberg's poem "Howl" is the subject of a much-publicized obscenity trial in San Francisco in 1956, beginning a mass migration of disaffected young people to the bohemian city by the bay. Post-Sputnik, *San Francisco Examiner* gossip columnist Herb Caen complains about the influx of "Beat" characters into his North Beach neighborhood and coins the term "Beatnik," creating the diminutive of Beat by playing off the name of the Russian satellite "Sputnik" and implying that the Beats are "out of this world." Thereafter "Beatniks"—a label which quickly sticks in the public mind—are associated with every anti-establishment, juvenile delinquent, commie, and rock and roll hoodlum type in America. The iconic image of a beatnik is a beret-wearing bongo drummer sporting a Fidel Castro beard.

Lacking a category for street musicians and radical individualists such as Coleman, "Calypso Joe" becomes "Bongo Joe" and Joe a hapless member of the "Beatniks," although he will say in years later if anyone inspired anyone, he inspired the "Beat Generation," not the other way around.

In the summer of 1958, Pat Kirkwood, a Van-Dyke bearded beatnik character who dabbles in sculpture and dresses out in a motorcycle jacket and boots, brings his Daddy's boat down from Fort Worth to Galveston for some fun on the island. After a day on the water, he strolls the Seawall and is inevitably drawn to the unusual booming sound of Joe's drums. He instantly knows what to do with him: Kirkwood is opening a beatnik coffee shop and after-hours speakeasy he's calling the Cellar, and Joe's crazy sound is just what he needs for the club. Wait till Big Mike and Charlie Whomper and all the gone cats in Fort Worth get a load of this guy, he thinks. Joe is hesitant, averse to nightclubs, but Kirkwood is persuasive and they settle on Joe playing the Cellar during Galveston's off-season.

In September of 1959, Joe beats his way from Galveston to Fort Worth.

If Joe now sometimes gets overshadowed in the middle of this narrative, it's because his stage in Fort Worth is crowded, weird, and unexpectedly historical.

Fort Worth in 1959 has the image of a dusty conservative Cowtown on the high Texas prairies, Dallas' poor cousin. It's the last place in America you would expect to find a "beatnik" club. In fact, though, Fort Worth has long been an untamed frontier town just south of the buckle on the Bible belt, a place where the law sometimes looks the other way. Hell's Half Acre, as the lower end of town is known in the late nineteenth century, is a Babylon of two-story bars, cathouses, and dancehalls where cowboys straight off the trail drives brawl, gamble, and whore. This frontier spirit carries on at Camp Bowie, where men with less sense than courage learn to fly during WWI. In the 1930s a three-and-a-half mile section of Jacksboro Highway comes to be known as Thunder Road for all the commotion it creates. In its heyday, there are eighteen restaurants, six liquor stores, ten motels, and seven nightclubs—many of them with chicken wire over the bandstands to protect the bands from beer bottles thrown by dissatisfied listeners. Several businesses are fronts for gambling, and all are crooked places—no one comes out a winner.

Pat Kirkwood's father, "Pappy," famously runs the Four Deuces gambling parlor, a Spanish colonial style castle sitting on three acres at 2222 Jacksboro Hwy. Pat Jr. is born at the 2222 and grows up in a "strange environment," as he likes to say. "I thought everyone had a craps game going on in their front room." As a kid, Pat sits on the roof of the 2222 and rates the action by the number of ambulances that show up on Jacksboro Highway: two or three is a slow night; seven or eight and a lot of people are spending money on Thunder Road, or Jax Beer Hwy, as it's variously known. Cab drivers get a $100 tip to bring rich oilmen staying at the Hotel Texas over to the Four Deuces. Suitcases of money are exchanged. A host of famous characters inhabit the place. Kirkwood sees his father and U. S. House Speaker Sam Rayburn go through a couple of quarts of Jack a day; Dick Kleberg of the King Ranch takes his turn at the cards alongside big game hunter Frank Buck. Lower-rung types such as a young hustler named Jack Ruby find their way there, too, although Ruby neither drinks nor gambles.

Kirkwood, Jr. is described by a friend as a "younger, taller wilder version of Pappy: deep-voiced, bearded, partial to automatic pistols, and when he laughs, he breaks into a teeth-gritting, devilish howl." During the 1950s, Kirkwood has a career as a stock-car driver. His Cadillac Coupe de Ville is always number 13, and as he races against a Chrysler 300 or Lincoln Sapri he wears a hood with devil horns—Kirkwood is the "villain" on the track and loves the role.

One day in the late fifties, rockabilly singer Johnny Carroll meets Kirkwood. Cleburne, Texas-native Carroll is the real deal and a couple of breaks would have made him the second Elvis. A 1957 photo shows 19-year-old Carroll with his hands on the shoulders of a very young Johnny Cash and Jerry Lee Lewis. The other Sun artists all hit a lucky streak and become stars while Carroll parlays a couple of small hits into buying an Airstream trailer which he takes on the road playing the teen nightclub and county fair circuit.

In 1958, he's on tour in Texas and takes some time off before a gig at a county fair to check out the nearby stock car races. Wandering through the pits a few hours before race time, he can't resist climbing behind the wheel of a car numbered 13. It's Kirkwood's car. Kirkwood's roughneck pit crew finds Johnny at the wheel all dressed up in his rockabilly costume, the word "faggot" is thrown around, and a fight breaks out. Kirkwood shows up just in time to save Johnny's profile from permanent damage. He looks Carroll up and down—Kirkwood is a villain but a sophisticated one with a taste for 1950s rebel culture—and introduces himself.

"Let's take a ride," he tells Carroll.

"I'm playing in 30 minutes and I'm already late," Carroll says.

"Well get in then," Kirkwood motions. Kirkwood drives Johnny in #13 at Deadman's Curve speed and right at show time, in dramatic fashion, Carroll jumps out of the screaming car and races onto the stage. Carroll and Kirkwood have become fast friends on the drive over.

One night, he and Johnny Carroll both sit in on an unlimited stakes poker game and Kirkwood wins a small property located below a hotel in downtown Fort Worth. It's Carroll who originally has the vision of "The Cellar." Downtown Fort Worth rolls up the sidewalks after dark, he points out, and it's almost an insult to the town's wild, anything goes, frontier heritage. He pitches Kirkwood the idea of an after-hours musician's nightclub where players can jam following their regular gigs. "Well," Kirkwood says, "I've been looking for a place to get everyone out of my living room at night."

It's Kirkwood who comes up with the idea of running the place under the guise of a "beatnik coffee house." Inspired by San Francisco's North Beach literary scene, the beatnik "coffee house" in 1959 has become a safe space for all kinds of emerging fringe activities—from stand-up comedy (a local radio host named George Carlin gets his start on the Cellar stage) to folk music to renegade poetry readings. *Naked Lunch* author William S. Burroughs says of Jack Kerouac, the King of the Beats and author of the Beat bibles *On the Road* (1957) and *The Dharma Bums* (1958), "Kerouac sold a million blue jeans and opened a thousand coffee houses in America." The Cellar, in 1959, would have to be one of the first. Kirkwood even claims the Cellar is the original "beat" coffeehouse of its kind, but he's showing his provincialism. The Purple Onion in San Francisco (Pucho's Purple Onion in Houston is an unauthorized spin-off) is a walk-down cellar, where a young black poetess named Maya Angelou performs. North Beach is full of bohemian dives such as The Hungry I, the Co-Existence Bagel Shop, and most aptly, The Cellar, where Ruth Weiss first reads her poetry accompanied by jazz in 1956. On the East Coast, the first "folknik" club, opening in Greenwich Village in 1957, is the Café Bizarre. It looks like a carnival spookhouse and features Vampira look-alike waitresses and a guy in a Frankenstein mask feeling his way around in the dark. Folk musician Dave Van Ronk opens for Odetta at the club's premier and can't understand why tourists equate the Village with *Tales from the Crypt*: "Bela Lugosi is weird, Greenwich Village is weird, therefore . . ." he thinks.

Kirkwood has probably never visited any of these haunts and therefore is somewhat justified in claiming he's created something new. Between the coasts, at least, from NY to San Fran, there's no place that even approaches the Cellar's weirdness—and that's its unofficial motto: "You must be weird or you wouldn't be here." The real genius behind the idea is more practical, though: by running a "coffee shop" instead of a regular nightclub he can stay open all hours and avoid the expense and hassle of maintaining a liquor license. Not that there isn't plenty of alcohol at the Cellar—it's just kept in a case under the cash register or in Kirkwood's car parked in the alley and doled out to VIPs along with set-ups sold by the house.

The original Cellar is located at 1111 Houston in

downtown Fort Worth and opens on September 24, 1959. "When this town curls up and dies, we start swinging," Kirkwood brags. Outside, so an opening night legend goes, two beatniks are standing in front of the Cellar, one with a cigar box.

> Beatnik One: "Hey, man, I didn't know you smoke."
> Beatnik 2: "I don't, man; I'm moving."

The club is straight out of the lyrics to Pajama Game observes an opening night reporter: a dark place where no one knows your face, you only see silhouettes, and who cares how late it gets. After hours on the sleeping streets of downtown Fort Worth the Cellar is the only place with a light bulb lit. It is a true walk-down, subterranean club. The atmosphere of the place is beatnik noir. Kirkwood requires his employees to wear all black (Kirkwood himself prefers a black turtleneck) and there are the requisite bearded beatnik types such as "Big Mike" Calloway, Pete "The Hero" Gill, and bouncer Charlie "Whomper" Williams. Kirkwood and his crew, many of them his old pit crew leftover from his stock-racing days, paint all the walls black and stencil white slogans on the wall: "Evil spelled backward is live," "Coffee Jazz and Thou," "Swingeth with us and thou shalt learn to dig." There's a row of tables along a wall for the older crowd, but the main space is left open with throw pillows for beatnik-style seating. The pillows are always catching on fire from dropped cigarettes or getting stained by vomit so Kirkwood sprays them down with a new product he's heard about—Scotchgard.

The real draw of the place, though, isn't the beatniks; it's the waitresses. Waitresses at the Cellar don't dress for work, they undress, stripping down to their cotton panties and bras and picking up a drink tray. Some of them are as young as 16; one blonde wears a jewel in her naval. Many a Texas Christian University co-ed pays her tuition waitressing at the Cellar.

The Cellar opens at 6 pm and attracts an early crowd of young beatniks and those wanting to get a glimpse of one in Fort Worth. A folk musician strums from the stage. Occasionally some kid gets up and reads his "Howl"-inspired dipshit beatnik poetry. But after hours, when the other bars close at midnight and the theater goers from nearby Casa Mañana are looking for a nightcap, the Cellar becomes the city's protected hideaway for an older, late-night crowd, which includes not only the thrill-seekers hoping the waitresses will take their tops off but also all the powerbrokers in Fort Worth. Mayor Tom McCann is a regular. Off-duty cops are also regulars. Reporters from the *Fort Worth Star-Telegram*, politicians, and visiting VIPs all drink free, but it's under the table. The signature drink is grapefruit juice spiked with a heavy pour of Everclear—pure grain alcohol. For the un-hip, Mr. Sam, the black man in the kitchen, mixes flavored drinks with McCormick's rum flavoring, almost no alcohol content. Set-ups are provided and patrons in the know bring their own bottles.

Beyond the speakeasy liquor and long-legged north Texas girls in their underwear, however, the Cellar's long-term legacy (until the club closes in 1972) is the music coming from the bandstand—eclectic, jazzy, original, and most of all loud. Kirkwood wants the music to be heard two blocks away when the entrance door is closed. He wants it so loud that the patrons can't hear themselves talk and no one can say, "Hey, why don't we go somewhere else." All thanks to a Fender Dual Showman 100-watt amp and two 15-inch JBL Lansings pointed directly at the audience.

The original 1959 line-up, brought out on a two-hour rotation that starts at 6 pm and often ends at dawn, is folksinger Jack Estes, bandleader Johnny Carroll, and Joe. Known as "Calypso Joe" in the tropical climes of Galveston, he is inelegantly re-christened by Kirkwood with the moniker "Cannibal Joe" for his Cellar gig. Joe also has to wear black, earning him a second nickname from his white employers—"Shine." Joe is African black, his skin completely unreflective, and dressed in black against the black walls in the semi-darkness sometimes all you can see of him, so it's said, are his white teeth. He is always smiling.

Folk musician Jack Estes caters to the early crowd made up of kids brave enough to descend the stairs into the darkness. Jack's a kid, too, 19 years old and originally from Waco. He grows up listening to Bob Gibson, The Sons of the Pioneers, Pete Seeger, and Woody Guthrie. Hank, Sr. is the next best thing to Jesus for him and is his inspiration to learn how to play guitar. In 1957, Jack is at the University of Texas in Austin studying acting when the first folky coffee houses open on "the Drag" across from the University. Sipping bad coffee at Jester's Café with a friend, he borrows a patron's guitar and casually starts strumming and singing. "Sing louder" someone says, and the next thing he knows he's a regular performer.

Austin is full of interesting students who are artists and musicians and writers, but all the college professors have to offer is "memorize this." It's a generation that leaves school to actually learn something, that hits the road, and so does Jack after a year at UT. He's formed a folk trio and he and the other guys head to Dallas. When they reach the "Y" north of Waco where the road splits and poses a fateful question—Dallas or Fort Worth?—one of the guys says, "Hey, there's a good coffee shop in Fort Worth," so they veer left, and that's how Jack becomes one of the original Cellar Dwellers.

The Cellar is unlike anything Jack has ever seen. Most coffee houses at the time are places where some guy is up there on the stage plucking nylon strings and singing ninety-eight verses of "Lord Randall My Son." At the Cellar, though, there is total freedom—you can play whatever you want and say whatever you want. If you want to scream "Fuck it!" do it, free and wide open. The money is poor—ten dollars a night is what Kirkwood pays him—but that's enough to cover three meals and the fringe benefits are excellent: if you can't get laid at the Cellar, you are really lame. The waitresses are wearing hardly anything, Jack marvels—you can almost see their kitty feathers.

Jack plays folk selections but starts to throw in some bawdy songs which become his bag:

> *A nymphomaniacal Alice*
> *used a dynamite stick for a phallus*
> *They found her vagina in South Carolina*
> *and her rectum in Buckingham Palace.*

Or

> *There once was a woman from Exeter*
> *All the men would turn their necks to her*
> *She once was so bold as to take out and wave*
> *The external parts of her sexeter.*

Every time he does one of these songs someone in the crowd comes up afterwards and says, "I got one for you." Soon he can go eight minutes of his set with dirty limericks.

Johnny Carroll takes over as the crowd roughens up later in the evening. Carroll, the self-titled "musical director" at the club, can sing as well as Elvis and is a consummate showman who works out intricate dance steps with his bandmates. He still dresses in fifties j.d. jeans and a t-shirt, but he no longer exclusively plays rockabilly. Now he plays what he wants to play and won't take requests. He might just as likely play "Where Have All the Flowers Gone?" as he will "Honey Hush" by Big Joe Turner, or a Tex Ritter song after covering Carl Perkins. He can play a deafening version of "Malagueña" that brings the crowd sitting on the pillows to their feet. Cellar Dwellers love to echo his cries of "Hey Bo-Diddley" as Carroll scratches out the chords on his Danelectro guitar while playing a bass drum and high-hat cymbal with his feet.

And then, following Carroll, out walks onto the stage a tall black man keeping Johnny's beat on a pair of 55-gallon oil drums and Carroll shouts, "King George Cannibal Jones, take it away!"

Joe hits the barrels with a frighteningly powerful force, his drumsticks 18-inch links of steel pipe with rubber crutch ends for tips. He's strapped metal Bandaid cans filled with BBs to the steel rods that make it sound as if he is simultaneously drumming and rattling. Joe can play the drums forty-five minutes solid with little effort, a feat which astonishes the other musicians and especially the college kids in the audience who are studying music at North Texas State in nearby Denton. No one has ever quite heard the rhythms he finds in the oil-can drums, part Calypso, part Bo Diddley beat, part bebop jazz, as well as an occasional martial beat left over from his Officer's Club show days during World War II. He can whistle piercingly loud between the large gap in his front teeth and the whistled notes often fade into off-key jazz chords—like a Charlie Parker solo, but weirder, otherworldly. He comes out of the hot jazz, bebop jazz era and is less like Cab Calloway than the much wilder Slim Gaillard. Joe is also a consummate mimic of animal sounds—barking dogs, crowing roosters, even dinosaurs dying at the onset of the ice age—and can create a range of human voices, most notably a wild, comic female falsetto. Every now and then he improvises a story, playing on audience members, or says something spontaneous and philosophical. Listeners such as Jack Estes can tell he's a ruminative if self-educated man.

On the big oil drums, he plays with real feeling, producing deep, deep rhythms that surge and transform into a sound far more sophisticated and complex than the typical booming rhythms of the time. He is something totally different and new—"a combination of ancient fertility rituals and modern nuclear bomb tests," as one Cellar visitor says. For fun, Pat Kirkwood tricks the Fort Worth Star-Telegram's very square, very sober music critic and high school Music Teacher of the Year, E. Clive Whitlock, into coming down to the Cellar to review one of Joe's early performances.

Whitlock is apparently left speechless and never files the review.

Sometimes very late at night Joe puts down his drumsticks and takes a turn at blues and jazz standards on a beat piano in the corner, playing only the black keys, it's said. He sits in on piano and drums with the other bands and also backs up the demanding Johnny Carroll.

About a year after the club opens, Jack Estes hits the road for Greenwich Village in New York City and Carroll expands the bandstand to include some side musicians: he famously doesn't hire bands; he hires musicians. The first musician he hires at the new club is a teenaged kid named Arvel Stricklin, Jr. Stricklin, like Kirkwood, grows up off Jacksboro Highway. He lives next to the Skyliner Ballroom, a club with a retractable roof, and on pleasant, clear nights Arvel hears great black performers such as Jimmy Reed, Howlin' Wolf, and Sonny Boy Williamson through his open window. That sets his musical taste. He meets Johnny Carroll when he's barely in his teens and is going with a girl who is president of the Johnny Carroll fan club in Fort Worth. When he's fifteen, he takes a girl on a date to the just-opened Cellar in early 1960. The waitress brings them a coke and Kirkwood introduces himself to the kids and pours a healthy shot of whiskey in their cokes. Kirkwood is a perfect gentleman and when they finish their cokes he orders one of the waitresses to bring them another round. Again, he tops it off with whiskey.

Stricklin spends the next 12 years at the club, starting off as a drummer for Johnny Carroll, but Carroll hears him play guitar during a break one day and puts him at the lead of an un-named trio that goes into the rotation at the Cellar. On drums is a kid named Eddie Pace, who shows up at the Cellar frequently with a pair of bongo drums but can also play a trap set. Rip Stokes, a bouncer for the club, aspires to be a bass player and Carroll gives him the chance to be one in Stricklin's three-piece. It's before the British invasion and they play cover versions of black Top 40—Otis Redding,

Bobby Blue Bland, BB King. Black Top 40 is popular in the white clubs but since the bandstands are rarely integrated you need white players who can play that music. Stricklin is a Jax-Beer-Highway-raised white blues boy, a natural. That was Arvel, Delbert McClinton, Doug Sahm and a few others at the time. The Cellar does have an integrated band, though, unique in Fort Worth and much of Texas. In addition to Joe, there's Billy Robins on sax and Chester Freeman on drums.

The bandstand is integrated, but not the club.

Kirkwood has a strict unwritten policy of "no blacks allowed." He doesn't like to think what would happen if a Negro came on to one of the white waitresses in a crowd full of Fort Worth cowboys. A sign at the entrance to the club applies only to blacks or anyone else they don't want inside: "The Cellar Has the Highest Cover Charge in the World: 1000 dollars." Kirkwood always says that if a Negro wants in the club badly enough to pay the ten Cs he'll close down the club and have a private party for him.

The black musicians at the Cellar, such as Joe, have their own small dressing room off the stage, separate from the dressing room for the white performers. After closing time, Joe sleeps there. There's a couch, some chairs, and a little TV.

With the best musical line-up in the Southwest, near-naked waitresses, a big bottle of amphetamines under the cash register, and contraband liquor poured with a heavy hand, the place just can't be stopped. In fact, it's too much fun; dangerously fun. It's pretty common for someone to over-indulge and get out of line and do something unacceptable such as slipping a bowling ball grip on one of the waitresses. Before you know it, there's a fight and Cellar workers might find themselves out the back alley facing down a gun barrel. Kirkwood's philosophy when it comes to fighting is don't send one man, send six—"All Hands on Deck." For such occasions, the kitchen has a rack filled with knives, brass knuckles, and slapjacks for the crew. Pat Kirkwood himself joins the fights, up to his ass in cowboys, grinning like the devil.

One evening the TCU football team shows up looking to beat up some beatniks. Included is a player who is later drafted into the pros. But the Cellar crew sends three of the boys to the hospital.

Another night, an out-of-towner who doesn't know about the under-the-table liquor set up, orders a glass of the club's legal rum-flavored drink—Mr. Sam knows the exact ratio of flavoring to put in so as not to exceed the legal limit. The out-of-towner gets belligerent when he thinks the club is watering down drinks and ends up hitting a bouncer with a folding chair. Arvel Stricklin is in the middle of it, responding to the all hands on deck call, and gets punched in the face and is momentarily blinded. When he re-focuses he sees a funny look on the out-of-towner's face, a look of surprise: from the bandstand "Cannibal" has thrown a rubber tire hammer and clocked the guy in the head.

In addition to crowd control, Joe does a little of everything around the club, filling in on piano when needed, even sweeping up—labor which he characteristically turns into a performance piece. Joe's gotten hold of a simulated sound toy, marketed by Mattel, called a "V-rroom!" It looks like a small motorcycle engine with an ignition key and switch and can be bolted on a tricycle or bicycle. The thing is really loud when turned on—sounds like a motorcycle gang coming down on top of you. Joe has the idea to bolt it to the push-broom he uses to clean up around the club. When there is an accident, glass broke or some other mess after a fight, he runs out into the crowd pushing his V-rroom! broom, the little engine whining out. It becomes part of his act and the club shines a spotlight on him as he races to clean up spills. Joe is constantly modifying junked radios, telephones, and other primitive electronics and creating novel devices such as the V-rroom broom. At the Fort Worth Stock Show Parade one year, he pulls up at the very end pushing a shopping cart with a stick pony rocking inside it. A sound device in a suitcase loudly plays a recording of a horse whinnying. It's a hit.

In 1960, the Cellar is swinging, and it's an election year. The young Catholic senator John Kennedy runs against Eisenhower's VP, Richard Nixon. At the 1960 Republican Party convention held in Chicago, Illinois, former President Herbert Hoover, 85 years of age and in his sixth decade of attending these conventions, takes to the stage accompanied to the tune of "Happy Days Are Here Again" and declares that America is in a "frightening moral slump" of crime, juvenile delinquency, and corruption. And who is to blame? "Communists, eggheads, and beatniks." "During the 14 years since the war," he tells the conventioneers, "communist conspiracies and their fronts have poured the Marxist poison into our people. They insist that love of country, pride of a people in their history, their ideals, and their accomplishments, is wicked nationalism. Ever since the war, the communist fronts and the beatniks and the eggheads have conducted a national chorus of denunciation of this wicked nationalism." Beatniks are bums and communists, and if your hair isn't military short and your tie tightly knotted, you could be one.

Even the youthful John F. Kennedy (he's 42) has the label of "beatnik" slapped on him—by none other than Ayn Rand, who publishes an article in the Bible of the conservative movement, *Human Events*, titled "J.F.K—High Class Beatnik?" Rand's September 1, 1960 article is a response to Kennedy's "New Frontier" speech, a decidedly youth-oriented one that, in the tones of a counter-cultural indictment of the status quo, asks young Americans to make the choice "between the fresh air of progress and the stale, dank atmosphere of 'normalcy'—between dedication or mediocrity." Who is Kennedy? Rand asks. Is he a bright young man, or is he "the figure of an irresponsible young beatnik, a high-class beatnik, who, with unlimited means at his disposal, chose the power game, as others choose hot-rod racing—for kicks."

Accepting his party's nomination in a speech delivered

Did Beatniks Kill John F. Kennedy?

September 14, 1960, Kennedy, who appears to read a lot of his own press, responds to Rand and the other writers who have labelled him "the farthest-out liberal democrat around" by saying, "While I am not certain of the 'beatnik' definition of 'farthest-out,' I am certain that this was not intended as a compliment."

Never one to miss an opportunity to publicize the club, Kirkwood rides the election year wave and converts the daytime cellar into the "headquarters" for a slate of "Beatnik" candidates including "Big Mike" Calloway and Peter "The Hero" Gill, who run for local offices in Fort Worth. Both men sport goatees, Raybans, and berets. At their Cellar-sponsored campaign rally in downtown Fort Worth, a banner reads, "Kick the cows out of cowtown and let the cats in to swing." Peter campaigns on a platform of "free espresso, dancing ladies, and beatniks all over the place." Mike promises to improve the conditions in flophouses for winos. In 1960, Fort Worth Mayor Tom McCann signs a proclamation declaring "National Beatnik Week" in Fort Worth and *Life* magazine runs a photo of the mayor signing the proclamation flanked by Kirkwood, Peter "The Hero," and an "unidentified" woman who looks like a Grecian Goddess in a white flowing dress.

Kennedy, the "beatnik," wins the election of 1960 by the narrowest of margins. Frank Sinatra supports Kennedy along the way, singing a rendition of his 1959 hit "High Hopes" at rallies with lyrics altered to fit the campaign. Frank and all the rest of the Rat Pack are invited to the inauguration, with the exception of Sammy Davis, Jr. Sammy has had the effrontery to marry a white woman, a Swedish-born actress named May Britt, and he's *persona non grata* in 1960. Frank gives his inauguration tickets to Speedway Café owner Biaggio DeAndrea, an old friend from his down and out Galveston days who let him put bowl after bowl of chili on his tab.

Kennedy's administration promises to be everything Ike's wasn't: young, forward-looking, stylish, and (under the influence of his wife, Jackie) artistic. A poet, Robert Frost, even reads at the inauguration ceremony in January of 1961. It genuinely feels like the beginning of something new.

The Cellar is re-born, too, after a series of police raids. The "gestapo," as Pat Kirkwood calls it, starts clamping down on the Cellar. Every teenager in Fort Worth who has gotten in trouble seems to mention the Cellar. The police report over a hundred incidents in the past couple of years—one woman interviewed for the Fort Worth paper claims the club and its environment led directly to her teenage son's death. Vice Squad Lt. Oliver Bell calls the Cellar a "public nuisance." "I think Lt. Bell is the squarest . . . a right kind of cat," replies Kirkwood, then adds, "Man, like, if all the young cats came here said they did, we'd need a hole in the ground like with an H bomb. These young cats are messing around some other place and moan to the home magistrates that they are digging at the Cellar." In fact, Kirkwood himself has summoned the cops to report disturbances dozens of times: each visit by the cops produces a newspaper headline that only increases his business.

Joe continues to play the Cellar during the cold winter months of Galveston's off-season. In February of 1962, on a bitterly cold night, the Melba Hotel burns down on top of the Cellar. The cause of the fire, which is reported at 4 am, is "unknown." Normally, there would still have been a crowd at the Cellar, but the city has again temporarily shut down the club over "health" violations. Prior to the fire, witnesses see piles of Kirkwood's Scotchgard-ed pillows in the stairwell. The fire follows an elevator shaft to an upstairs record shop which drops a mass of flaming wax into the nightclub when the rafters collapse.

Another downtown subterranean location is quickly found at 10th and Main and opens in late March of 1962. The ceilings in the new place are low—8 feet high and 3 feet of smoke. The walls are painted black again, the slogans go up, and the place keeps going without missing a beat of Joe's drums. Carroll even finds another out-of-tune saloon piano for George to play the black keys on. Word is the place is "neater" and "cleaner" than the old one, but no one's sure if this is a recommendation. One beatnik is known to iron his shoelaces for the grand re-opening; another is rumored to have bathed. Overheard at the New Cellar: "I never knew he drank until he came to work sober."

The Cellar is now popular enough for Kirkwood to expand to other cities—Houston, Dallas, and San Antonio. The San Antonio Cellar, or the "Cellar del Sur," opens in 1962 on Kirkwood's favorite memorial disaster day, December 7, Pearl Harbor Day. Fort Worth patrons who visit down south comment that it's "much larger than the original hole in Fort Worth." The club kicks off with a performance by Little Lynn, an ivory-skinned woman who affects a less voluptuous Marilyn Monroe look and is one of Kirkwood's Fort Worth Cellar waitresses. She's eighteen but already has a hardened look about her, definitely not one of the girls working the Cellar to pay her TCU tuition. Little Lynn and Joe, who is known as "Animal Jones" in S.A., make the club a hit and soon as many as 2000 patrons—mostly servicemen from nearby military bases—are paying a dollar a head to get in on a Saturday night. It's a rowdy place, fights breaking out regularly, and "Animal Jones" calms the sometimes out of control crowd by pounding on the heads of patrons with his drum mallets. Little Lynn celebrates her birthday there and Kirkwood and the gang give her a pearl-handled pistol. They don't bother to tell her it doesn't have a firing pin. Soon thereafter, Jack Ruby, who's known Kirkwood since the 4 Deuces days and is now owner of a Dallas striptease club, The Carousel, recruits Little Lynn away from the Cellar and hires her as a topless dancer.

In spite of its success, or because of it, the Cellar del Sur doesn't last long, going dark after four months. There's only so much late-night cash to be spent in downtown San Antonio and the honkytonks and beer bars on Houston Street feel the pinch caused by the packed "coffee house" run by bearded out-of-towners. Someone calls the cops in early January and reports a phony murder at the Cellar. In Fort Worth Kirkwood can turn such incidents into good publicity, but not in San Antonio. On February 10th, the Provost Marshall at Fort Sam Houston places the club off-limits to military personnel, citing "excessive arrests of military personnel, extremely dim lighting, and unsanitary conditions of patrons sitting or reclining on cushions on the floor." "Dubber" Simms, a former bouncer in Fort Worth and now the San Antonio Cellar's manager, scoffs at the charges: hell, there have only been 26 arrests at the club since December, the cushions are sanitary, and the lights aren't dimmer than the lights in other San Antonio bars. But by March 30th, the club is beat down. "The military has killed us dead," Dubber says. Local entrepreneurs immediately step in and announce they will open their own beatnik club called "Little Jack's Inferno," featuring a "satanic decorum" and leotard-clad waitresses. The club, a bald-faced re-creation of New York's Café Bizarre, will cater to "plush beatniks" says Little Jack. "Ain't no such animal as plush beatniks," snorts Dubber. By early May, the Cellar bongos have been packed up and the Cellar crowd has all disappeared or left town.

Towards the end of the San Antonio club's four-month run (the club goes dark on April 24) a little "beat" guy shows up and asks Dubber, "Is there anything I can do around here to make some food money?"

Dubber appraises the little guy as one of the "brokes" who frequently come around the club looking to make a few bucks. "You can do some pearl diving," he says, and shows him a pile of dirty dishes. The little guy—he's five eight and 140—stays on for a day or two. His name is Lee, and the girls in the club remember him because he never tries to hit on them—which is decidedly odd—and prefers, instead, to stare at the soap bubbles as he washes dishes.

Lee Harvey Oswald, of Fort Worth, has a lot to think about reflected in the soap bubbles as he earns enough scratch to return home: he's recently lost his job in Fort Worth, and a few days prior to turning up in San Antonio, he's tried to assassinate a retired U.S. Army General at his home in a tuney Dallas suburb.

Originally from New Orleans, Oswald is a misfit kid who starts reading Karl Marx when he's twelve. Barely seventeen, Oswald follows in an older brother's footsteps and in 1956 enlists in the Marines. His fellow Marines nickname him Oswaldskovich after he proselytizes Marxism with them. In October of 1959, Oswald is granted a hardship discharge to take care of his mother in Fort Worth, but instead, just before his twentieth birthday, he defects to Russia: he wants to see how a communist government operates firsthand. Two years of life in Russia, however, convince him it's no better than the U.S., plus it has no bowling alleys. In the summer of 1962 he returns to America, settling in Fort Worth with his Russian bride, Marina, and their infant daughter.

Back in the U.S. of A., his "unwanted" discharge status from the Marines makes it difficult for him to find and keep a job. He's appealed his status to the Secretary of the Navy, John Connally, who is now running for Governor of Texas, but Connally ignores him. "I received an honorable discharge and then those bastards in the Navy changed it into an undesirable discharge . . . And Connally signed this undesirable discharge," he tells a friend. Service industry workers at Jack Ruby's Carousel Club in Dallas, which Oswald visits, overhear him badmouthing Connally.

Oswald has a reputation in these circles for being a none-too-bright crank and someone who could easily be manipulated. The truth, however, is that in spite of being a high school dropout, Oswald is deeply knowledgeable about Marxism and about American history, particularly America's meddling in the affairs of foreign countries in Asia and Central and South America. He speaks Russian fluently, a fact that astounds his very cosmopolitan Dallas friend George de Mohrenschildt. He and de Mohrenschildt, who moves in Dallas' circle of European and Russian emigres, discuss politics and world affairs. On several occasions, he tells de Mohrenschildt how much he admires the new President's civil rights agenda. He remarks on "how handsome" Kennedy looks "and what open and sincere features he has and how different he looks from the other ratty politicians." He is also an outspoken admirer of Reverend Martin Luther King. Oswald has grown up in New Orleans and witnesses firsthand America's cancerous racism and passionately believes all people should be treated equally.

If there is an antithesis to Kennedy and King it's the anti-communist pro-segregationist General Edwin A. Walker. Walker's "Code Pink" anti-communist indoctrination of his troops in Germany is so rabid that President Kennedy is forced by the troops themselves to ask for Walker's resignation in 1961. *Time* magazine puts the pariah-ed General on its cover with the headline, "Thunder on the Right," and Walker becomes the face of far-right conservatism in America.

In forced retirement, Walker moves to America's most conservative large city, Dallas, Texas, home to radical right-wingers such as the anti-clerical Baptist preacher Reverend Criswell and staunch anti-communist (and richest man in the world) H. L. Hunt, an oil baron. Six thousand supporters welcome Walker at the City Coliseum on December 12, 1961, and the mayor of Dallas hands him a short-brimmed hat and declares him an honorary Dallas-ite. From Dallas, Walker continues his crusade. His views are so radical that even some on the far right distance themselves from him.

In September, 1962, three months after Lee Harvey Oswald arrives in Fort Worth, Walker travels to the South and incites riots as the University of Mississippi attempts to admit its first black student, James Meredith. On the radio that day Walker sounds crazy, babbling about "the conspiracy of the crucifixion by anti-Christ conspirators." Attorney General Robert Kennedy has him arrested and confines him to a mental hospital for ninety days (he is released after five). Walker returns to Dallas welcomed by a crowd waving

Confederate flags and signs reading "Walker for President 1964."

Lee Harvey Oswald has been watching these affairs and tells his wife Marina that Walker is "the head of America's fascist organizations." In late March of 1963, Oswald loses his job in Fort Worth. He's also just bought a rifle by mail.

You can't miss Walker's Dallas home on Turtle Creek with its giant American flag or, on some occasions, Confederate flag waving. Oswald stashes the rifle in some brush near the home on April 7. On the night of April 10, he retrieves the gun, stakes out Walker as he does his taxes in his office, and fires a bullet through the window. The bullet disintegrates after knicking the wood frame between the upper and lower window casements. Walker still has wall plaster in his hair when the police investigate the attempted assassination. He's apparently bulletproof.

George de Mohrenschildt sees Oswald the day the news breaks of the attempt on Walker's life and jokes with Lee, "You missed him Lee." Oswald is disturbingly quiet—the two often joke with each other—and doesn't laugh. Later, Marina sends de Mohrenschildt and his wife a picture of Oswald holding the rifle he used in his attempt to kill Walker. On the back of the photo she writes, in Russian, "Ha Ha! Lee Harvey Oswald, killer of fascists!" "I would be willing any time to fight these segregationists—and to die for my black brothers," he once tells de Mohrenschildt.

Kennedy has made civil rights a central plank of his election platform in 1960, and a few weeks after the country watches Sheriff Bull Connor's attack dogs "go to work" on student protestors in Alabama in May of 1963, he delivers on radio and television the most important speech of his presidency, "The Civil Rights Address." "We are confronted primarily with a moral issue," he begins. "It is as old as the scriptures and is as clear as the American Constitution. One hundred years of delay have passed since President Lincoln freed the slaves, yet their heirs are not fully free. . . . Now the time has come for this Nation to fulfill its promise."

Kennedy has been privately and in smaller ways acting on these beliefs for some time. At a presidential event on April 30, 1961 held in Chicago's McCormick Place, a young black Secret Service officer working out of the Midwest office named Abraham Bolden draws bathroom detail. Normally a Chicago policeman would guard the bathroom, but Bolden, one of a handful of black secret service agents, is used to such undignified posts. Still, he's disappointed. "Jiminy," he thinks as he hears Hail to the Chief playing, "I'll never see the president from down here." But a group loudly talking descends the staircase into the bathroom and a moment later John F. Kennedy walks in with an entourage including Chicago's Mayor Daley. Bolden remains respectfully quiet, not greeting the President by name, but Kennedy walks right up to Bolden and asks him, "Are you one of Chicago's finest or with the Secret Service?" Dick Jordan, one of Kennedy's personal agents, answers for Bolden and tells the president his name and confirms he is a secret service agent. Kennedy smiles a very nice smile and asks the room, "Have there ever been any Negros on the White House detail?" He's looking at Bolden now, and Bolden replies, "Not to my knowledge, Mr. President." Kennedy, eyes glittering, looks to Mayor Daley and then asks Bolden, "Would you like to be the first?" "Yes sir, Mr. President," Bolden answers. Kennedy says he'll look forward to seeing him soon and walks back up the steps to give his speech.

Kennedy keeps his word, and Bolden finds himself in the very white world of the White House Secret Service detail, most of whom are Southern-born. Bolden hardly fits in this good old boy club. On one of Bolden's first assignments guarding the President at his family home in Hyaniss Port, Bolden's supervisor, Harvey Henderson, half-lit and opening another beer, tells Bolden privately, "I don't care what the President thinks of you. You're a nigger. You were born a nigger, you'll die a nigger, never be anything but a nigger, so act like one." They put him on the boat trailing Kennedy's yacht on Nantucket Sound and he's drenched by the spray coming off the stern. An apparently watchful Kennedy takes note, however, and the next day Bolden is on-board the yacht and is invited to lunch with the President and First Lady.

Back in D.C., Bolden hears the agents on more than one occasion say that if someone tries to shoot the President, they aren't going to take a bullet for him. Bolden is shocked at the loose behavior of the agents when they accompany Kennedy on trips. The agents get drunk, hire prostitutes, and fail at their duties in numerous ways.

In July of 1962, Bolden reports these events to Chief James Rowley, head of the Secret Service, detailing the laxity of the Secret Service detail and their hatred of Kennedy. It isn't all of them, he tells Rowley, but there are a few who are unqualified to be anywhere near the President of the United States. His reports are ignored, he is treated like a stool-pigeon, and after only four months on the White House detail resigns his post and returns to the Chicago office.

Because of his civil rights agenda, Kennedy knows he will lose every southern state in the 1964 election. He can't afford to lose Texas, too, and embarks on a five-city tour of Texas. The third stop on the tour, after stays in Houston and San Antonio, is Fort Worth. He spends the night at the Hotel Texas, two blocks from Pat Kirkwood's Cellar and within earshot of Joe's drums.

On November 20, 1963, the first day of Kennedy's Texas tour, Cellar guitarist Arvel Stricklin, Jr. goes to see a daytime rehearsal of the Shrine Circus at Will Rogers Coliseum in Fort Worth. Some of the circus performers have been hanging out at the Cellar after hours and they give him a press pass. The feature act is the famous high-wire-walking Wallenda family. In January of 1962, two members of the family have fallen to their deaths while constructing a seven-man pyramid on a high-wire, with no net. For their performance in Fort Worth Karl Wallenda announces they will perform this dangerous formation one last time. An NBC film crew is on hand to film the stunt for the "Dupont Show of the Week." *Life* and *The Saturday Evening Post* also send reporters.

At the rehearsal, Karl Wallenda says encouragingly, "Come on Suicide Squadron," as the troupe approaches the high wire strung thirty-six feet above the floor of the Coliseum, eye-level with the building's art-deco arches. Watching the rehearsal that afternoon, Arvel Stricklin sees the Wallendas tightrope walk out to the middle of the Coliseum and begin forming the "Seven High."

Suddenly the lights go out across the Coliseum, leaving Stricklin and other audience members gasping in fright for the performers.

The lights are out for nearly a full minute. Stricklin hears sharp German whispers from the wire. When the lights come back up, somehow, even in the dark, the Wallendas have managed to form the pyramid. Back down on the arena floor, the members of the Suicide Squadron shakily light cigarettes and curse under their breath.

Stricklin, like everyone else, is relieved, but when the lights brighten he finds his eyes are focused on a puzzling feature of the Coliseum: up in the rafters, about six stories up, Stricklin sees a plywood platform big enough for a man to stand on. It never figures into the high-wire act nor supports any lights or other hardware as the show continues. This strikes Stricklin's showbiz instincts as odd.

A clown act follows the "Seven High" and it features the old gag of stuffing a dozen clowns inside a tiny car. This car is different, though. It's in the shape of a long limousine with the top down, just a plywood cut-out on either side, painted black, and it moves slowly across the arena floor with clowns, crouched down impossibly low and dragging this contraption, suddenly appearing from behind it and coming over the top. A couple of days later Stricklin can't help but think that the clown car looked like the kind of limousine a visiting dignitary or president might ride in a parade.

The Wallendas perform the "Seven High" without mishap that night and the circus performers celebrate at the Cellar, where they are entertained by "Cannibal," The Arvel Stricklin Trio, Johnny Carroll, and the waitresses. It's as if the Circus went to the Circus. The place is full of roustabouts, make-up-less clowns, beautiful trapeze artists, midgets, animal handlers, and sideshow barkers, giving the club an even more Fellini-esque feel than usual. The NBC news crew covering the Wallenda's final performance has also made it to the Cellar. They've asked their boss if they can stay in Fort Worth a few more days to cover an event apparently less newsworthy than the Wallenda's retirement of their infamous pyramid—President John F. Kennedy is arriving in Fort Worth on November 21st for a series of minor campaign events in Fort Worth and Dallas. They don't get footage of the Wallendas falling to their death—always the hidden hope when covering a dangerous circus stunt—but they can double-dip and maybe something important will happen during Kennedy's visit. One of the Shrine circus clowns, Happy Keller, hearing that Kennedy will be staying nearby walks the two blocks from the Cellar to the Hotel Texas, hands the desk clerk a Goldwater sticker, and asks him to post it in the President's mailbox.

The next morning, after the party on November 21st, Stricklin wakes up sometime around noon and turns on the radio. During the local newsbreak, he hears a story about gunshots reportedly coming from inside the Will Rogers Coliseum early that morning. Shrine officials explain the incident by saying that Circus sharpshooters had been sighting their guns. Stricklin sips his morning coffee and again thinks something is odd: only newly-purchased guns need to be sighted. Gun stores are everywhere in Dallas and Fort Worth, being frontier towns. All you need in order to buy one is to ask with a smile and some cash. Just down the street from the Coliseum, high-powered rifles, scopes, even collapsible rifles can be bought at a local gun shop. The radio news program next gives details about President John F. Kennedy's upcoming visit to Fort Worth and his overnight stay at the Hotel Texas, after which he will travel to Dallas to give a speech at the Trade Mart.

Before Kennnedy's plane arrives in Fort Worth, his

advance team is busy making preparations. Jeb Byrne is Kennedy's man on the ground in Fort Worth. He has to deal with everything from coordinating a Chamber of Commerce breakfast on the morning of November 22 in the Ballroom at the Hotel Texas to seating arrangements for the delegation—which includes Lyndon Baines Johnson, (now) Governor John Connolly, and Senator Ralph Yarborough—as they travel by motorcade from the Hotel Texas to Carswell Air Force Base in Dallas. It's a little trickier than it sounds because Johnson and Connolly can't stand the liberal Yarborough.

He's also in charge of making sure all of the campaign events and audiences are integrated. But trouble starts almost immediately. One of Byrne's advance team members is a Negro, and the hotel staff informs him he'll need to stay in a Black's Only hotel. Byrne and his superiors make a call on the ground: if the Negro advance team member can't stay, no one in the Kennedy party will stay at the Hotel Texas. Overnight, the Hotel Texas is now an integrated hotel. (It's one of those small, forgotten events happening during that time in towns across the South that are still clinging to aspects of Jim Crowe.) Alarmed by the hotel's policy, Byrne now looks over the guest list to the Chamber of Commerce breakfast.

"Will there will be any blacks in attendance?" he asks a Union representative who is helping with the logistics in Fort Worth.

"There will be damn few unless somebody does something," the representative tells him.

"How many black people live in Tarrant County?" Byrne asks.

70,000, he's told.

"Well can someone give me the name of a leader in the black community?"

Soon he's on the phone with Dr. Marion Brooks, who gives him forty names to put on the guest list. It's now an integrated event.

Did Beatniks Kill John F. Kennedy?

The day before the breakfast, Byrne receives a call from the Tarrant County Sheriff: "I've got a deputy here named Jake Cardenas who heads the local unit of the Political Organization of Spanish-Speaking People and they're hurt no one's involved them in the breakfast."

He puts Cardenas on the line with Byrne, who tells him, "I didn't think of it."

Cardenas replies, respectfully but resignedly, "No one ever does."

Byrne feels like kicking himself all the way back to his home state of Maine. He's able to find ten tickets for the Latinos, though, and Cardenas later picks them up.

Kennedy lands at Carswell Air Force Base at 11:07 pm. The crowd of five thousand is separated from the taxiing Air Force One—a gleaming red, white, and blue sight in the spotlights—by 200 yards of police tape. Law enforcement is stationed every five feet along the tape. The large crowd cheers Kennedy as he walks down the gangplank, but Jackie Kennedy, thirty-four years of age and wearing a black Persian lamb suit with a box jacket, white kid gloves, and double-knotted pearls with matching earrings, is greeted like the true celebrity. It is her first visit to Texas and her first public appearance since the death of their son, Patrick Bouvier Kennedy, who dies from a respiratory illness just three days after his birth in August of 1963. The President is holding his son's hand when he dies.

The president looks tan, reporters note. Jackie's brown hair is lighter in person than in photographs.

The Air Force band from Barksdale Air Force base in Shreveport plays ruffles and flourishes and "Hail to the Chief." Kennedy confounds his secret service agents by shaking hundreds of hands stretched out beyond the police tape.

He finally enters a limo and travels by motorcade to the Hotel Texas in downtown Fort Worth. Signs along the motorcade are almost all positive and even witty: Students from North Texas State's Young Democrats hoist signs saying "Kennedy in 1964" that flipped around read "Goldwater in 1864." Another large crowd is gathered at the Hotel Texas and Kennedy again surfs through it, shaking hands. The hotel lobby, one reporter remarks, "sounds like an echo chamber."

The Kennedys stay in the second-best suite in the hotel, room 850 (comped by the hotel manager at $75 dollars/night), while Vice-President Johnson and Ladybird stay in the larger and better accommodated $100/night Will Rogers Suite on the 13th floor. This is not a snub as some in the Press interpret it: a large office building faces the Will Rogers Suite and the Secret Service doesn't have the manpower to secure it. Suite 850 has two bedrooms, and a group of local art collectors have decorated them with original works, some of them masterpieces. By arrangement, the first couple sleep that night in separate bedrooms. Mrs. Kennedy is expected to stay in the room with French works by Claude Pendergast, Claude Monet, and Rauol Dufy, but the President's special 5-inch-thick horsehair mattress—he has a permanently injured back—will only fit in the room intended for Jackie. So it's Mrs. Kennedy who sleeps beneath Thomas Eakins' nude swimmers. The next morning the couple does a double-take when they realize the paintings in their rooms are originals, not prints.

The Press, that night and the morning of the 22nd, are not allowed access to the eighth floor, which is guarded by Secret Service and local firemen. A reporter phones Vice-President Johnson and invites him for a drink at the nearby Press Club. Johnson says he's tired and has work to do, but in fact, he is hosting his own gathering.

President Kennedy orders a pot of coffee from room service at one o'clock in the morning. He's not quite ready for bed, it appears . . .

It's the beginning of the night's "vigils" for the Secret Service. The agents are hungry and they need strong drink. Sometimes they don't even wait to get the President put away and start their drinking on the plane. The agents decide to leave the fire department in charge of the President's security and see what downtown Fort Worth has to offer.

The Secret Service agents first begin drinking at a nearby bar called the Press Club. Normally the bar only serves until midnight but management breaks the rules and keeps pouring until almost 1 am. A young TCU student and cub reporter named Bob Schieffer (future CBS News Anchor) is there and excited to be around the White House Press Corps members, men with famous bylines such as Robert Pierpont and Tom Wicker. At closing time one of the Secret Service agents is introduced to Schieffer and *Fort Worth Star-Telegram* reporter Phil Record, who, the agent is told, can escort them to a notorious after-hours drinking spot, the Cellar. Waitresses in their underthings? Liquor for a wink and a nod? Even Lyndon Johnson has been invited to the "party" there that night by his Texas mistress, Madeleine Brown. Schieffer and Record—who frequently writes about Cellar antics in the *Star-Telegram* and is always comped his drinks there—know that whatever the agents might be looking for it could well be there.

The agents can hear the place a block before they enter, Joe's drums banging as loud as gunfire. Schieffer points the suits down the stairs, cigarette smoke rising from the subterranean entrance, and the agents walk heavy-footed beneath the $1000 cover-charge sign. Dubber looks them over at the door and since they're in suits motions them to the tables in the corner.

The place is so packed that night a floor man has to push through the crowd ahead of the waitresses trying to deliver drinks. A couple of Jack Ruby's strippers are there, including the Marilyn Monroe-esque Little Lynn who used to waitress for Kirkwood. The NBC cameramen are there as well.

The musical set that night alternates between Arvel Stricklin's trio, "Cannibal Jones" on his oil drums, and the Johnny Carroll Band. It's a mix of blues, black Top 40 hits, and the occasional Johnny Carroll wildcard number such as "The Lady is a Tramp." Joe plays his forty-five-minute set then hangs out with the other black musicians in the break room.

The crowd is as large as Stricklin has ever seen it inside the Cellar. There are a lot of unfamiliar suits in the place, out-of-towners. Kirkwood notices and asks Dubber who they are. Dubber shrugs and says some of them have been there since before midnight. They're drinking from their own bottles and hitting on the lingerie-clad waitresses, but that's why you come to the Cellar. It's nothing unusual, but Kirkwood goes over to the waitress who is serving the strangers.

"They're Secret Service agents," she says, wide-eyed.

"How do you know?" he asks her.

"They showed me their badges," she giggles. "I even held one."

Later, Kirkwood and Johnny Carroll hear one of the agents casually say, "We got bored and asked the fire department to stand guard outside the President's hotel room." An NBC cameramen recognizes the Secret Service and starts to set up a shot of the scene that night but an agent sees him and says threateningly that no cameras are allowed. The reporters are used to such verbal abuse from Kennedy's Secret Service Agents. That morning, though, one of the cameramen has had enough and goes around the corner from the club and makes a phone call to a national columnist, Drew Pearson.

"Guess who's drinking at 2 am in a beatnik nightclub in Fort Worth?" he begins.

The most remarkable story that night, however, more remarkable than Secret Service agents getting drunk and misbehaving (which they continue to do to this day), is told by Joe to his friend Helen Glau of San Antonio sometime before his death in 1999, and she makes a brief mention of it when interviewed for Joe's obituary in the *San Antonio Express-News*. Here Joe's own life story significantly intersects with the President's death.

"Cannibal," the story goes, is on break in the little room

reserved for the black performers at the Cellar. Joe gets along well with his fellow black performers and although he is well-liked and even respected by his white bosses and fellow performers he doesn't really talk openly with them nor socialize with them. The black and white world of Fort Worth Texas in 1963 is very much a black and white world. It's startling, then, when one of the suits walks into the Negro dressing room and displays his Secret Service badge. Does Joe know that the President is in town? He doesn't. "Bring your drums," he's told. "You're going to play a private concert." Joe checks to see who is on stage and seeing he has a least a couple of hours before his next set, loads his drums on a wheelbarrow and follows the agent. They head the two blocks to the Hotel Texas.

The official record of that final morning of the President's life says that Kennedy arrives at the Hotel Texas around 11:50 am, is tired, and goes to his suite on the 8th floor, while Jackie Kennedy sleeps in a separate suite next door. Upstairs, Lyndon Baines Johnson and his Texas cronies are holding a party (he's decided not to go to the crowded Cellar). Although the President says he is tired and ready to sleep, apparently he isn't and orders a pot of coffee at 1 am. A big part of the historical record of John F. Kennedy's presidency—his after-hours and off-the-record exploits—does not appear in any official document of the time.

And in the grander history of these events, George "Bongo Joe" Coleman is the perfect musician to entertain Kennedy that early morning of November 22, 1963.

Joe and the President are hardly peers, but they are born into the same Post-WWI world; Joe in 1923, Kennedy in 1918. Both serve in the military during World War II. Although they might seem to inhabit different worlds, in some ways Kennedy inviting a musician from a beatnik nightclub to play for him is completely in character. Kennedy is President of the United States, but he's also our most subterranean of presidents. The kind of after-hours club where Joe plays is the natural habitat of his performer friends such as Frank Sinatra, as well as Kennedy's string of mistresses. LBJ's mistress, Madeleine Brown, sometimes has drinks at the Cellar. The President's behavior is famously reckless. He has an affair with mobster Sam Giancana's moll and is romantically linked to Marilyn Monroe, teen-aged White House interns, and the ex-wife of J. Edgar Hoover spook Cord Meyer, Mary Meyer. Mary claims to have obtained a supply of LSD from Timothy Leary to "turn-on" the most powerful men in Washington. She makes love to Kennedy while both are tripping, she says, and under the influence of the hallucinogen he has an epiphany about de-escalating the nuclear arms race with the Soviet Union.

Although Kennedy stays in his hotel that night and doesn't visit the Cellar, it's not impossible to imagine him right at home among the "weird." The "freaks" sense some sympathy from Kennedy. The man is an outsider, after all—a Catholic in a Protestant land. He is tolerant, apparently, of difference. In Mexico City, June 1962, Kennedy's motorcade is halted by a man who the Secret Service agent in charge, Gerald Behn, says "had the appearance of a typical beatnik." When the beatnik comes around to Kennedy's side of the car, Behn hits him and knocks him down. Kennedy reportedly blows up over this incident and reprimands the agent for hitting the beatnik.

Kennedy also knows something about the Beat Generation. Frank Sinatra's butler recalls hearing Sinatra and Kennedy discussing the Brazilian wax sported by actress Juliet Prowse. "A naked lunch is just what I want," Kennedy jokes to Sinatra, although the reference to the still-banned-at-the-time William S. Burroughs novel is lost on the Chairman of the Board. Jackie Kennedy is at least as hip as her husband. During the 1960 campaign she is photographed by Jacques Lowe reading *The Dharma Bums* (1958)—Jack Kerouac's handbook for how to "drop out" of society. She tells *Reader's Digest* she reads everything from "Colette to Kerouac." Kerouac once casually mentions to his editor Ellis

Amburn that he has lunched with Jackie at the White House, but when Amburn asks his friend Jackie about meeting Kerouac she coyly refuses to confirm or deny the meeting: "We asked many writers to the White House."

The Kennedys' taste in literature and their personal style is remarkable enough in some corners of America to brand them as suspiciously unconventional. Jack dresses cool: he wears turtlenecks, just like Steve McQueen. The fact that Kennedy doesn't wear a hat at his wintry inauguration and his brother Robert often doesn't wear ties at meetings upsets some people in 1960. Robert Kennedy, according to Ben Bradlee, looks like a "Brooks Brothers Beatnik." When Jackie wears a sleeveless sundress to a Good Friday service in Palm Beach, everyone thinks "it was a little too free-thinking and beatnik," recalls *Vogue* editor Hamish Bowles.

It would not be completely out of character, therefore, for the President to request a performance by a fringe performer at a beatnik club such as Bongo Joe. Perhaps, somehow, the President knows they have a mutual friend, Sammy Davis, Jr.?

Joe's Story: He is brought from the Cellar to a room that has been cleared in the nearby Hotel Texas, asked some questions by the Secret Service agents, and showed where to set up his drums (or perhaps there is a piano there for him to play). After the room is secured, the President walks in and takes a seat. Joe looks around the room in the hopes that Mrs. Kennedy is there, too, but she's not. Joe plays for about half an hour for the President of the United States; the set list is lost now. If he is on piano, Joe plays his blues set in F#, a medley of whatever tunes fit the inspiration of the moment. If he is on drums, he plays his signature original rhythms, pausing occasionally to philosophize, whistling between his teeth, improvising lyrics. If the President is listening closely he hears a catalog of snippets of Americana music they have both grown up with, leaning towards big band and jazz melodies from the 1930s and 1940s, but also traditional songs popular in the first half of the twentieth century.

Joe's favorite songs are Erskine Hawkins's "After Hours" and Woody Herman's "Blue Flame" and he references jazz standards such as "Flyin' Home" and "Night Train" and some Duke Ellington, mixing it all up with "Mammy's Little Baby Loves Shortenin' Bread" and "Pop Goes the Weasel." If the last concert you hear in your life as President of the United States is a private set by Joe, you wouldn't complain: Joe's a pure product of America. After the show, the President gets up, thanks Joe, and chats with him for a bit. He has an easy manner with African-Americans that betrays no condescension. Still, it is a sight—Bongo Joe, black as the night outside, dressed in his all-black Cellar uniform, and John F. Kennedy, the most powerful man in the world, taking a private moment away from all that, taken out of that world by this unique performer who somehow ends up being the last performer President John F. Kennedy will ever hear.

Joe later writes down his memories of the performance for posterity or perhaps proof. No one knows where that piece of paper is anymore but it is read by a close friend who believes him. Joe has never been known to make up stories. He has no reason to do so.

After playing for Kennedy, he takes his drums back to the Cellar where he is due to perform another set. The Secret Service agents are starting to pack the place now. They all hear Joe that night. He's part of everyone's soundtrack album of the last day of Kennedy's life.

The agents drink until nearly sunrise even though some of them have an 8 o'clock wake-up call. At one point, an agent flashes his Secret Service credentials to impress a waitress or perhaps Jack Ruby's stripper, Little Lynn, and then misplaces his badge. At 5 am, the remaining agents stagger up the impossibly long and steep stairs into the grey/black dawning of November 22, 1963 on Main Street. They're smashed on Salty Dogs laced with Everclear. It's two blocks back to their rooms at the Hotel Texas where they must sober up before that morning's duty—escorting the president from the Hotel Texas by motorcade at 10 am to

Did Beatniks Kill John F. Kennedy?

Carswell Air Force Base, where Kennedy will fly to Dallas for another motorcade procession through downtown.

Kennedy wakes around 7 am and will be working on about 4-5 hours sleep that day. The kitchen has been waiting for the President's breakfast order and a phone call arrives from room 850: he'll have a large pot of coffee, a large orange juice, two eggs boiled five minutes, toast and marmalade. George Jackson, a tall negro who is a veteran waiter at the hotel, takes a breakfast cart up the service elevator to the eight floor. "Man," he says, shaking his head the entire trip to the President's room, "I have never even seen a President of the United States. Now I'm going to walk right into the room with him." When he arrives on the eighth floor and pushes the cart into the hall a Secret Service agents stops him, lifts the covers off the dishes to inspect them, looks under the cart, then studies Jackson up and down. He nods towards room 850. There another Kennedy handler appraises him and gives him an orange pin to wear on his white waiter's jacket. Jackson pushes the cart inside the foyer and into the small living room to the right where the President is sitting. "Good morning, Mr. President," he says, and Kennedy returns, "Good morning." Kennedy is chatting with one of his advisers, Kenny O'Donnell. Jackson returns to the foyer but pauses, moves close to Kennedy's valet, George Thomas, and asks him, "Is there any little thing I might keep as a remembrance of serving the president today?" Thomas smiles, walks into the living room and politely interrupts the President with the request. Kennedy reaches in to his jacket pocket and walks to the foyer and gives Jackson a PT-109 tie clasp, shaking his hand.

Later, Jackie Kennedy joins him in the living room, and they talk about the heartening reception they have received in hostile political territory the night before. "You know," he tells her, "if someone wanted to kill me last night, they could have just walked up to me with a pistol and shot me."

For the morning speech, the public enters the Hotel Texas parking lot from 9th street. 8th is blocked off between

Main and Commerce and all traffic stopped. The Tarrant County Sheriff's Posse, led by Sheriff Lon Evans, guards the event. A steady rain falls, the crowd umbrella-ed and wearing hats. It hasn't rained in a while—Kennedy has broken the drought! Ten-year old Ben Proctor has a camera and tall Kenneth Clark offers to hoist him up on his shoulders if he'll share the photos with him. A Carter-Riverside High student group has brought a ladder to get pictures of the event but police don't allow it. John Lenox takes off work to see the President's speech: He saw FDR in 1936. By 8 am, there are 4000 people in the crowd despite the rain, including some black faces, though not as many as desired by the advance team. Dubber and Charlie Whomper are in the crowd, too, having walked the two blocks to the hotel after the last Secret Service agent has finally left and the club closes down. They both carry pistols, as they routinely do while working the Cellar, but they are no danger to the President.

Joe is in the crowd, too. No street performer would miss such an opportunity: there is a large, empty, beckoning stage and thousands of people in front of it. An hour or so before the President's appearance Joe hoists his oil drums onto the stage in front of the Hotel Texas, where the President will speak, and begins to drum and sing, perhaps emboldened by the early-morning private concert. On view in public now, he is quickly and rudely removed by Kennedy's handlers. However, if you look closely at the footage of the crowd watching Kennedy's early-morning speech in the rain there are a few, very few black faces in the crowd, and one of those appears to be George "Cannibal Jones" Coleman.

Kennedy takes the stage in front of the 4000-strong crowd around 8:30 am and gives a brief speech extolling Fort Worth as the site of many important Cold War defense-industry plants. He is the only man on the platform not wearing a rain coat in the weather. "Ladies and gentlemen," he begins, "there are no faint hearts in Fort Worth, and I appreciate, I appreciate, your being here this morning. Mrs.

Kennedy is organizing herself, it takes longer, but of course she looks better than we do when she does it." The line is a popular one, and he delivers some version of it at every speech he gives on the Texas tour. "But we appreciate your welcome. This city's been a great western city, the defense of the west, cattle, oil, and all the rest. Fort Worth, as it did in World War II, as it did in developing the best bomber system in the world, the B-58, and as it will now do in developing the best fighter system in the world, the TFX, Fort Worth will play its proper part." Probably only a few people in the crowd know—and they are mostly on stage with the President—that the contract for the TFX (later re-named the F-111) has been secured for Fort Worth's General Dynamics plant by the manipulations of Lyndon Baines Johnson, who reportedly walks away from the deal with $100,000 dollars in cash and a plum for the Kennedy re-election in Texas.

Doors open at 7:45 am for the Ballroom Breakfast that will follow Kennedy's speech, and early guests are treated to the sounds of the Jimmy Rovitto Combo. Dining room captain Wayne Mitchell places red flowers at the center table where the President will sit; he's so busy he doesn't even see the huge crowd. As the ballroom fills up it's a sea of all-white faces, but a spokesperson for the Chamber of Commerce denies, the night before, that "no Negro citizens will attend the breakfast." They have been invited, but he doesn't know if any of them purchased their tickets.

Before attending the 9 am gathering at the Hotel Texas' ballroom, Kennedy changes into a dry coat and is thus ten minutes late for the breakfast. The local broadcaster covering the event live on Dallas/Fort Worth TV thus has a long segment to fill. He does so in an eerily precognizant way, discussing the President's security team and, oddly, the McKinley assassination of 1901, which he describes in such detail it's as if he's reading from a history book:

> When President Kennedy appeared outside in
> the parking lot he broke one of the cardinal

rules of security, in fact he broke it two or three times, he went out in the crowd, and of course the Secret Service men find this the most nervous time of a Presidential appearance. As long as the Secret Service can keep the crowd away from the President they have a good chance of protecting him, but once he moves into a crowd the Secret Service men are nearly immobilized in protecting him. Another rule is that anyone who approaches the President should have both hands visible and empty. In a crowd there's no way of determining that, so whenever the President does move out into a crowd for handshaking and backslapping and exchanging of pleasantries, he is always at the mercy of the crowd and the Secret Service is at its least effective position. On September 6, 1901, those two rules were broken and it ended in tragedy. That was the day President William McKinley was appearing at the Pan American exhibit in Buffalo, New York, and at a public reception the crowd moved in around him. The three Secret Service men who were guarding him had no chance to screen the people who were approaching him. Because it was a hot day, Secret Service agents allowed people to have handkerchiefs in their hands to wipe their perspiring brows. It just so happened that one of the men in the crowd was an unemployed millworker. He said he was an anarchist; he was also a man with a long history of mental illness. And as on many important occasions in the world, no one sensed that anything was going to happen. When McKinley reached out to shake his hand, it seemed like a familiar scene, the

> President of the United States shaking the hand of Fred Nobody. The assassin shattered that picture quickly. He slapped away McKinley's hand and fired two shots point blank. In an instant, McKinley's attacker was driven to the floor. As the President was being helped to a chair, McKinley murmured, "Don't let them hurt him." Seven days later McKinley was dead. Oddly enough the assassination attempt was staged in the temple of music, quite an ironical note, and there was a quiet Bach sonata being played in the background when the two fatal shots rang out. Now here comes Vice President Johnson . . .

It seems everyone knows Kennedy is going to be assassinated except the President himself.

The Eastern Hills High School Band plays "Hail to the Chief" when JFK and Jackie arrive in the Ballroom; someone with an ironic sense of humor shouts "Ole!" The Texas Boys Choir then sings "The Eyes of Texas." Jackie, wearing a pink two-piece wool suit and matching pillbox hat, is applauded more loudly than the President. "Our hearts and our arms are open to you," Chamber of Commerce President Buck begins, and proceeds to introduce the guests on stage, who pop up and down in their seats to applause. When the President finally stands to deliver his breakfast remarks, he quips, "I know why everyone is so thin, having gotten up nine or ten times." In his remarks, Kennedy addresses the festering Vietnam War: "We would like to live as we have in the past, but history will not permit it. No one expects our life to be easy, certainly not in this century." Both John and Jackie are given pairs of boots by Buck, who adds kindly, "We won't ask you to put them on here."

For the ride to Carswell Airforce Base, where the President will fly to Dallas, Kennedy and his entourage exit the ballroom through the kitchen entrance on 8th Street. A crowd has been tipped-off and gathers. Donald C. Bubar, a Fort Worth attorney and member of the "Chamber of Commerce Sports Committee" elects to aid the Secret Service in Fort Worth and stands by the 8th Street door of the hotel, where limos are idling, waiting for Kennedy and his entourage. Bubar's an attentive and suspicious man and spots a character with a goatee standing near the ropes that are holding back the crowd. It's Charlie Whomper. "He's obviously a beatnik," Bubar thinks and edges towards the man. A Fort Worth policeman joins them. "Here to see the President?" Bubar asks Whomper, who mistakes him for a Secret Service agent. "Hey man, I saw a bunch of you guys last night down at the Cellar, like relaxing." Out of earshot of the beatnik, Bubar tells the cop, "The Secret Service was probably down at the Cellar trying to memorize the faces of all the queer individuals down there . . . a wise precaution."

From the Hotel Texas, the motorcade travels up Main Street to Bonant to Jacksboro Highway to River Oaks. A thousand kids at the River Oaks Elementary School cheer the procession. Then it's on to Roaring Springs and Carswell Airforce base, where the President boards a short flight to Dallas. He lands at the south end of Love Field, disembarks, and travels by motorcade through the streets of Dallas. The motorcade passes friendly supporters waving signs but also opponents. In reference to Republican candidate Barry Goldwater, one protestor carries a sign reading, "Let's Barry King John." He stops twice en route to converse with some Catholic nuns and with school children. The arranged route takes the Kennedy train down Mockingbird Lane, right on Lemmon Avenue, right at the "Y" on Turtle Creek Blvd, straight on Cedar Springs Road, left on North Harwood Street, right on Main Street, right on Houston Street, and then a sharp left onto Elm.

The shooting starts just after he makes the left onto Elm Street.

The little "beat" character who did some pearl diving at

the San Antonio Cellar is firing from a gunman's nest on the Sixth Floor of the Texas School Depository Building.

But Oswald isn't trying to shoot Kennedy at all. None of Oswald's acquaintances ever hear him utter a word against Kennedy. In fact, he thinks Kennedy has the chance to bring peace to the world and go down as America's greatest president.

Instead, his target is Texas Governor John Connally. It's Connally, now Governor Connally to boot, who rejected Oswald's request to have his discharge status changed from "unwanted" to honorable. The Connally who speaks out against Kennedy's civil rights agenda, calling it a threat to America's "sacred" private property rights. Oswald the devoted Marxist hates guys like Connally. His shot goes awry when he tries to kill General Walker. This time he hits his target, but there's collateral damage.

He sights the mail-order Mannlicher from his nest on the sixth floor of the Texas State School Depository building and fires a still undetermined number of times. One bullet enters Connally's back, exits through his chest, passes through his right wrist, and finally embeds in his left thigh. But the shooting doesn't stop. Even near-mortally wounded, what Connally hears is more than three shots, shots fired so rapidly it sounds like an automatic weapon to the military veteran and experienced hunter. There's other gunmen shooting from a grassy knoll opposite the book depository—a crossfire Arvel Stricklin later concludes are bullets fired by Sicilian gunmen disguised as Shrine Circus roustabouts, the same ones who had sighted their rifles a few nights earlier at the Will Rogers Coliseum. One of these assassins takes out the President's skull. Connally, who lives, sees fragments of brain matter land in his lap. For the second time, Oswald fails at an assassination attempt but succeeds at becoming, in his own words, "a patsy" in the murder of John F. Kennedy.

The gunfire momentarily freezes Secret Service agent Clint Hill, who then runs to JFK's car; Jackie Kennedy is sliding out the back on the convertible's trunk. It's all recorded in a 486-frame film shot by dressmaker Abraham Zapruder. The film has no soundtrack, but if it did . . .

Now there's a bunch of fiction but no science after that, as Bongo Joe sings. *There's not two sides of a question, there's every point on a compass and backwards and forwards. Everyone already knows everything and you don't want to be the one left out. Who knows? The Shadow knows. (Mad laughter). And he who laughs last laughs best. You've got to keep it cool and not act a fool. (Falsetto screams heard). It's a dog eat dog world. The guy with his name on the deck of cards doesn't even know the rules, makes them up as he goes along. And if you see a pitbull with a baton, well, maybe he's going to protect you, who knows. The next day's a terrible hangover, some of us get over it, some don't. (Sounds of dinosaurs dying in distress to the tune of "When the Saints Go Marching In").*

The very first suspect in the shooting is a Negro man who starts running after he hears the gunshots. He's running to pick up his little girl and shield her.

Dallas Police Department Officer Joe Smith is heading towards the Texas School Book Depository when an hysterical woman sees his uniform and yells, "They are shooting the President from the bushes." Smith reconnoiters the Elm Street extension, his gun pulled, and steps onto the grassy area off the street. Calm and erect, there is a man in a black suit on the knoll. Seeing Officer Smith's drawn gun he pulls out a credential badge. Officer Smith has seen Secret Service badges before and this one is real. The Secret Service "agent" leaves the scene, and history—he's never identified.

Arvel Stricklin, Jr. goes home that morning after working all night in the Cellar, skipping the President's speech in Fort Worth. He sleeps until noon, and then turns on the TV in time to hear the President is dead. As the details of the motorcade and of the shots coming from the sixth floor of the book depository emerge over the next twenty-four hours, Stricklin flashes, queasily, on the clown car and mysterious high platform in the Coliseum he's seen a few nights before, along with the story he's heard about gunshots in the Coliseum in the middle of the night.

When Pat Kirkwood hears that Kennedy has been killed, he puts his hand on his forehead and says, "Oh my God here we go." He loads up three girlfriends and leaves town, headed for Laredo and the Mexican border. He knows at some point he's going to have to answer a bunch of questions about the Secret Service drinking at the Cellar that night. Later, he's told about Oswald working the San Antonio Cellar, and that's another headache.

That night, Jack Ruby darkens the Carousel Club out of "respect," he says. At the Cellar, though, it's business as usual, but everyone is despondent, quiet, going through the motions. I mean, the president has been killed in our town, man. That lasts one night; the next everything goes back to normal.

Hearing of Kennedy's death, Frank Sinatra shuts himself in a room for three days and weeps.

Cellar alum, Jack Estes, is in New York the day of the assassination and is singing that night in a Greenwich Village coffee house. He's in the middle of a song about a racehorse called "Stuval" when he suddenly realizes the next line of the song is, "It was a big day down in Dallas, don't you wish you were there." He thinks, "Oh shit, I'm gonna get lynched," and he cuts it off—imagine singing something like that in New York City where Kennedy is popular on the night he is killed. He can already see himself being dragged off the stage and down the street . . .

The day after the assassination, from his Chicago offices, Abraham Bolden and all other agents are required to turn in their Secret Service badges. There is only one possible reason for this and the agents know it: someone has lost their badge or had it stolen. In the next few days, Bolden hears rumors of the Secret Service's antics at the Cellar, of the agents flashing their badges to impress the semi-nude waitresses, the story of the "agent" on the grassy knoll spotted immediately after the assassination, and puts it all together.

On November 24, 1963, Lyndon Johnson declares to Ambassador Lodge that he will "not lose" Vietnam. By the end of the year, over 16,000 American "advisors" are on the ground there. The F-111, manufactured in Fort Worth, flies over 4000 missions during the war. Investigation of the cash LBJ received for pushing through the General Dynamics contract in Fort Worth is shut down the day after the assassination and is not re-opened until 1969, after Johnson leaves office.

Two days after the assassination, Jack Ruby pays a visit to the office of Dallas sportswriter Bud Shrake and tells him to stop dating his star attraction, Jada. He then goes to a Western Union office a couple of blocks from where Lee Harvey Oswald is being held and wires Carousel dancer and former Cellar waitress Little Lynn a small amount of money to help her make rent. After that, Ruby calmly walks the two blocks to the police station and mingles with the cops, who all know him. He overhears a reporter trying to recall the name of the communist-front organization Oswald started in New Orleans and corrects him: "It was called the 'Fair Play for Cuba Committee.'" When Oswald is pressed through the crowd, cameras flashing, Ruby shoots him fatally in the stomach. The murder is broadcast live on television.

Pat Kirkwood, sitting in the Cadillac Bar in Nuevo Laredo, sees Jack Ruby kill Lee Harvey Oswald on Mexican television. Ruby has been a guest at the Cellar and he has recruited strippers from Kirkwood's pool of waitresses, including Little Lynn. "Maybe we better go back to Dallas," Kirkwood tells the girls.

Oswald is shot at the moment that Kennedy's funeral procession and burial ceremony are just beginning across the country in the capital. Jackie Kennedy meticulously patterns the funeral after that of Abraham Lincoln, based on photographs from April, 1865. The catafalque on which Lincoln's coffin was mounted, known as "The Temple of Doom," is brought out of storage for the Kennedy rites. Kennedy is carried through the streets of D.C. on the same caisson that carried Lincoln. The flowers decorating the casket are picked that morning from the memorial magnolia tree planted on the south lawn of the White House grounds by Lincoln's Vice President, Andrew Johnson. Lincoln was the Great Emancipator, and Jackie wants Kennedy's legacy to be his push for civil rights.

A few days after the assassination, the story of the Secret Service agents drinking at the Cellar until dawn hits the newspapers in Drew Pearson's "Merry-Go-Round" column:

> Six Secret Service men charged with protecting the president were in the Fort Worth Press Club the early morning of Friday November 22, some of them remaining until 3 am. This was the same day Kennedy was assassinated. They were drinking. One of them was reported to have been inebriated. When they departed, three were reportedly en route to an all-night beatnik rendezvous, 'The Cellar.'

Two days later the Inspector General for the Secret Service, Gerard B. McCann, drives out to Pat Kirkwood's home and interrogates Kirkwood and Cellar manager Dick Mackie. The Feds have two items on their agenda: the Cellar/Oswald connection and the Secret Service's carousing at the Cellar.

Kirkwood explains the former as a "coincidence" and tells agents Oswald worked one day at the San Antonio Cellar, was paid, and disappeared. End of story. Regarding the party at the Cellar on the long morning of November 22nd, the agents interviewing Kirkwood and Mackie make their case more than plain: "The Secret Service has had its name blackened enough in all this, so when you are asked about this, we would very much appreciate it if you didn't mention they were drinking Everclear."

"That's right," says Kirkwood. "They were only

drinking grapefruit juice."

Everyone, top to bottom, lies.

At Jack Ruby's bond hearing on December 23rd, 1963, Little Lynn, former Cellar waitress recruited as a dancer by Jack Ruby, is called in to testify. She arrives wearing cat-eyed sunglasses and a fur-trimmed mid-length black coat, carrying a black handbag. She of course attracts the attention of the press mob as the cops part a path for her to the courtroom. When she is searched by court officers, however, they find the little pistol she has been given as a birthday present at her San Antonio Cellar performance. The pistol is displayed to the press before Little Lynn is hustled off through a side door and booked and fingerprinted, as the cameras flash. She washes her ink-stained hands in a public sink. "What she didn't know," Kirkwood laughs when he sees the news, "was that the pretty little gun didn't have a firing pin, and she couldn't have shot it if she wanted to."

Little Lynn is called again as a witness in the Ruby trial on March 6th, 1964. This time she wears a white maternity dress—she is six-months pregnant. She is in a hallway when seven county prisoners oddly choose that moment to stage a prison break. They are armed with razor blades and fake guns. Looking for a hostage, two of them run after Little Lynn. "Oh my God! They are after me!" she screams, and faints.

Later, in 1964, when she is asked by Warren Commission investigators who the "they" was, she tells them she meant the escaped prisoners who were after her. When pressed, however, she says, "No—well, it all goes back to where I used to work. I had already been threatened by Pat Kirkwood. We never got along too well because I told the police, the vice squad about him and identified some policemen that were being paid off by him and everything, then he hated me for what I had done."

In spite of the white maternity dress she is wearing at the Ruby trial, Little Lynn is anything but innocent. In fact, she has been an informant for the Fort Worth Vice Squad since she was sixteen or seventeen years old and is a known pill popper and suspected prostitute. Kirkwood knows she talks about the Cellar to the cops and has played cat-and-mouse with them for two years by planting false information on her.

Now, Kirkwood wants to make sure Lynn keeps her mouth shut: she knows too much about the Cellar's gray areas.

She tells the Warren Commission, "After I went to court, he [Kirkwood] says, 'I want you down here' and I said, 'Well, I'm not coming down.'"

"Well, I'll see you on the way to the club and I'll see that you never make it inside the door," she reports Kirkwood saying.

The investigators confirm that Kirkwood is the owner of the Cellar, but his threat against Lynn is never followed up on. Many years later, when the story comes to light of the Secret Service badge disappearing the morning of November 22nd, the number one suspect for having nicked the badge among those who knew her well (such as Arvel Stricklin) is Ruby's Little Lynn.

Now, the Warren Commission interviews 552 persons about what happened that day and the days before the assassination, making November 22nd, 1963 arguably the single most researched day in the history of the world. They interview cops, plumbers, strippers ("Is there a difference between an exotic dancer and a striptease dancer?"), everyone in every walk of life who has pertinent information, giving us an amazingly deep view of Fort Worth, Dallas, and America as a whole during this period. All of this investigating, though, has been rigged to lead to a foregone conclusion: Oswald acted alone. Any other theory will certainly bring to light a hundred secrets the government doesn't want the public to know, such as the fact that the FBI dropped the ball on Oswald, whom they had interviewed and were tracking, and that the Kennedy Administration was still actively trying to kill Fidel Castro (no one wants another Missile Crisis).

On the political left, there is the belief that the assassin must have been a crew-cut John Bircher type opposed to Kennedy's civil rights agenda. However, the Commission seems to make a concerted effort to portray Oswald as being what rightwingers had long warned was the real danger in America—the homegrown American communist, the threat from within.

If so, who better to play that role than the stereotypical subversive of the time—the "beatnik"?

Interview after interview by the Warren Commission reveals that even though the real Oswald is clean-cut, clean-shaven, and neat in appearance—he looks a little bit like Kevin Costner—numerous witnesses describe him as a "beatnik." In the days before the assassination, Oswald is sighted all around Texas—in Alice, San Antonio, Freer, and Pleasanton—and in most cases he is described as dirty and unkempt and fitting the stereotype of the beatnik communist. He is frequently seen by informants in the company of other beatniks. In Mexico City, for example, where Oswald is trying to obtain a visa to visit Cuba, he is spotted by two embassy employees with "two other beatnik looking boys." An eyewitness in Dallas who recalls seeing Oswald on a firing range just prior to the assassination also says he was with a man whose hair was worn in a "beatnik style." One of the most controversial informants, Perry Russo, who testifies in Jim Garrison's investigation while under the influence of sodium pentothal, claims to have seen Oswald at a party in New Orleans where the assassination was discussed, and that Oswald "looked like a typical beatnik, extremely dirty, with his hair all messed up, the beard unkempt, a dirty t-shirt, and either blue jeans or khaki pants on. He wore white tennis shoes which were cruddy and had on no socks." When investigators show Russo a picture of a clean-shaven Oswald, he asks them to draw a beard on him, then says, yes, that's him.

Even witnesses who do not report Oswald looking "dirty and disheveled," however, make it a point to clarify, unprompted, that Oswald "was not a beatnik," as a man who sat next to Oswald on a bus out of Laredo, Texas says. Apparently he is surprised that Oswald's neat appearance is at odds with his stereotypical notion of what the president's assassin should look like—a scruffy beatnik.

Accordingly, what worse place could there be for the Secret Service agents to spend all night partying than in a club full of beatniks? The Chairman of the Warren Commission, Earl G. Warren himself, asks this, incredulously: "Now, don't you think that if a man who went to bed reasonably early, and hadn't been drinking the night before, would be more alert to see those things as a Secret Service agent, than if they stayed up until 3, 4, or 5 o'clock in the morning, going to beatnik joints and doing some drinking along the way? It would seem to me that a beatnik joint is a place where queer people of all kinds gather anyway, and that the mere fact that these men did leave their post of duty might be an indication to someone that the President was not being protected, and might leave an opening for them to go there and try to do something."

No one on the Commission seems aware of the little "beat" fellow, Lee Harvey Oswald, working as Kirkwood's dishwasher in the San Antonio Cellar for a couple of days—no doubt to Kirkwood's relief and no doubt because of his "grapefruit drink" deal with the FBI.

The Commission never hears from Abraham Bolden, either. Not only does he know about the agents' reckless behavior and determination not to prevent an assassination, he also witnesses his superiors destroying evidence of other assassination attempts prior to Dallas. And he knows about the badge nicked that night at the Cellar. In an act of conscience, Bolden makes a trip to Washington in May, 1964 with the intention of contacting J. Lee Rankin, council for the Warren Commission. He is in a phone booth ready to call Rankin but notices another agent has quickly ducked into the adjoining booth in order to hear his conversation. The agent drops a dime on Bolden. On May 18th, prior to testifying, Bolden is suddenly recalled to his Chicago office and ordered to appear in the office of the US Attorney. His superior, Mr. Martinall, is waiting for him, and tells the shocked Bolden he is being charged with attempted bribery. Frank Jones, a well-known felon and convicted perjurer, is making the charges. "You can't be serious," Bolden tells the US Attorney. "Prove we're wrong," he's told. Bolden is denied an attorney and even food that day and is not allowed to make any phone calls from jail. After three trials, he is sent to prison on bribery charges and sentenced to six years.

He ends up in Springfield's notorious "Tomb," a psychiatric prison ward, where he is subjected to a horrifying regimen of psychoactive drugs intended to erase his memory of the events surrounding the assassination. Bolden, the first African-American appointed to the White House Secret Service detail, the man John F. Kennedy once introduced to Robert McNamara as "the Jackie Robinson of the Secret Service," spends three years incarcerated and the rest of his life trying to clear his name.

1964 is not 1963. Two major cultural events are blunted by November 22, 1963: The release of Stanley Kubrick's cold war comedy *Dr. Strangelove* and the release of The Beatles' *With the Beatles*. The release date of Kubrick's film is put off until April of 1964. It's far too prescient a film, written by Texan Terry Southern, who bases the character of Major Jack D. Ripper on Dallas' Edwin A. Walker. Major Ripper, a rabid anti-communist and closeted homosexual (as, it turns out, was Walker) initiates a first strike against the Soviet Union and sets off the end of the world. Real-life Texas cowboy Slim Pickens bare-backs the Armageddon bomb. Kubrick originally asks John Wayne to play the role, but the material is far too pinko for The Duke. One scene has to be overdubbed: Major Kong, instructing his airmen on the contents of their survival kits—which include prophylactics and women's silk hosiery—says, "A feller could have a real good time in Dallas with all this stuff." "Dallas" is changed to "Vegas," quite noticeably, in the overdubbed version released in 1964.

With the Beatles is released on the day of the assassination and predictably goes un-noticed. Two months later, though, 70 million Americans watch the Beatles (partly named in reference to the "beat" generation) perform on The Ed Sullivan Show, and "Beatlemania" helps lift the malaise on the country following the assassination. The accompanying "British Invasion" of musical acts from England occurs around the same time as the passing of the landmark Civil Rights Act of 1964, which prohibits discrimination based on race, color, religion, sex, or national origin. One of the few areas of equality that exists before that time is cultural: both black and white audiences embrace black music—rhythm and blues—and, in fact, it's white teenagers who buy most of the r and b records in America in the '50s and early '60s. Now, just as black Americans have finally achieved civil rights victories, the Beatles and second-wave British invasion artists such as the Rolling Stones, the Who, and the Kinks kill black Top 40 as the staple music played on radio and in American nightclubs such as the Cellar. Post-Beatles, all you hear is white British r and b, pop, and rock.

The Cellar follows the musical trend in a new location. Fort Worth's planned Convention Center lands right on top of the Cellar and Kirkwood, unthinkably, moves it to an upstairs location at 509 ½ Main. He's run out of downtown commercial buildings with cellars. Some joker suggests he call the new Cellar "The Attic," but Kirkwood says he'll just hang his Cellar sign upside down. The grand re-re-opening date is Kirkwood's traditional one—Pearl Harbor Day, December 7, in 1964. The new house band, The Cellar Dwellers, play mostly Beatles covers and other songs by British Invasion bands. Jim Hill, a rock and roller who sold porno in high school and worked the door at the downstairs Cellar, takes over management of the upstairs Cellar. The 1964 crowd is all scruffy kids in blue jeans and t-shirts. One of them defaces the old slogan of "Coffee Jazz and Thou"—putting an x over "Jazz" and freehanding "Rock". One thing remains the same—the $1000 cover charge sign.

Joe doesn't make the move to the upstairs Cellar. He disappears one day towards the end of the 1111 Houston location, just before the Main Street rock and roll club opens. He leaves behind a cryptic message. When the morning crew shows up to clean the joint, they find a trail of debris leading up the stairs and out to the back alley. The old upright piano Joe sometimes plays boogie woogie and blues on, hitting the black keys almost exclusively, has been completely disassembled and carefully laid out in a trail. Arvel Stricklin can't imagine an upright piano could have that many parts laid out over 60 feet. What was Joe's message? he wonders. Maybe he was looking for something in the piano? Maybe his message was: Johnny Carroll, you need a better piano. Maybe he just knows it's the end of something and walks right out of the club with the $1000 cover charge.

Joe forever leaves "Cannibal Jones" behind and returns to Galveston full-time with his lasting moniker, "Bongo Joe," playing the Seawall and any other odd gigs he can pick up. In 1966, he's playing nightly in a piano bar owned by Christie Mitchell, the eccentric brother of Galveston-born oil tycoons George and Johnny Mitchell. Christie "the beachcomber" Mitchell is Galveston's semi-official promoter of the Island, columnist for the *The Galveston Daily News*, and character collector. A Chicago newsman has told Christie that the last cities in America with real characters are San Francisco, New Orleans, and Galveston. And there's Bongo Joe, playing on the jetties as silvery trout breach the gulf waters and the pink granite rocks of the jetties glitter in the moonlight. A character indeed. Christie hires him to play drums and piano at his newly-opened, theme-crazy, Polynesian-styled bathhouse/restaurant/nightclub—"Christie's Beachcomber." A "talking dolphin" show featuring "Pete" and "LBJ" brings in the family crowd during the day. In the evening, twenty-eight Waikiki gas flames light an outdoor pavilion, windchimes playing the gulf breeze.

Joe wheels his drums over the pulverized shell parking

lot leading up to a pagoda-ed entrance to the nightclub and once inside has the rare opportunity to play on a finely tuned piano. He's so popular his gig goes on nightly through the late 1960s, Joe pounding the black keys, whistling, snatching blues standards, gospel music, and bebop jazz from the air, surrounded by bamboo, tiki figures, and nets. It's all pastiche but Joe is the real thing.

It's now the sixties proper, or at least what everyone means when they refer to the sixties. Beatniks didn't kill John F. Kennedy, but Kennedy's death and the political upheavals that follow kill the apolitical beatniks, who are now officially political and called "hippies."

Author Tom Wolfe writes in *The Electric Koolaid Acid Test* that the difference between beatniks and hippies can be defined in three letters: LSD. Joe sings about the changing times there on the Seawall in front of the kids who are now smoking dope and throwing parties across from the Seawall in huge abandoned and graffiti-ed concrete bunkers that housed defensive batteries during World War II. The hippies love this improvised number, perhaps picking up on its Vietnam War context . . .

> *What I like about the jungle is*
> *all them barks,* sings Joe,
> *and roots,*
> *and herbs,*
> *and berries.*
> *I could drink or eat as much as I want to.*
> *Didn't have to worry about no federal control and*
> *prescription and all that stuff.*
> *They served their purpose for two,*
> *ah, twenty thousand years.*
> *Two hundred years did a good job of keeping one of*
> *them a secret,*
> *til the Americans came over,*
> *bombarded,*
> *confiscated,*

brought it over here,
slapped a label on it,
called it LSD.

He concludes with a loud drum flourish that challenges the white noise of the surf.

That summer of 1967, a young graduate student from UT Austin, Patrick B. Mullen, records Joe on a portable Nagra player right there on Joe's windy, salty stage. It's the beginning of the "Blues Revival" period of folklore scholarship and the smart young white kids from the suburbs are fascinated by black musicians such as Joe.

The performer Mullen records that day has now evolved the act generations of Texans still remember. Joe wears suspenders and high pants, a baseball cap, and a sequined shirt. Sometimes he wears a World War I helmet. He transports his 55-gallon oil drums on a rack mounted on an orange bicycle painted with his lasting name: Bongo Joe. The bike has an umbrella strapped to it and a cannibalized radio speakers mounted on the front. Usually there is a stray dog Joe has adopted sleeping at his feet. Joe drums, improvises songs, and whistles through the radio speakers connected to a home-made microphone rigged from a "borrowed" pay-phone handset. An orange and green washtub matching his colorful drums serves as his "kitty." A regular listener who has traveled to Galveston to hear Joe tells the graduate student setting up his recorder that Joe is "a real clown."

To Mullen's discerning ear, Joe is mixing jazz standards such as "Night Train" and "After Hours" with traditional American songs like "Mammy's Little Baby Loves Shortenin' Bread" and "Pop Goes the Weasel." Like the true jazz bebop musician he is, Joe only uses these songs as his melody and freely improvises on the tunes. Occasionally, he uses a hammer to re-shape his barrel's drum head and find a new tone. His improvised lyrics, Joe tells the eagerly listening Mullen, come to him through a process of "rapid concentration" that takes place while he unconsciously works out rhythms on his drums. He even keeps drumming as he answers Mullen's questions.

As the quarter-inch tape rolls, Joe sings about the tourists on the Seawall, especially pretty girls strolling by, but he is also philosophical and political. Notably, he has been following Jim Garrison's investigation of the Kennedy assassination:

> *Read all about it.*
> *Want volunteers to enlist.* [drums].
> *To protect Jim Garrison.*
> *He know too damn much.* [laughs, drums].
> *Read all about it.*
> *Jim Garrison got a lead.* [drums].
> *Men wanted to enlist to protect Jim Garrison.*
> *He's in hot water.*
> *Read all about it.* [drums].
> *Read all about it.*
> *Christ made an attempt to come back to earth.*
> *Saw what was goin' on and changed His mind.*
> [drums].

There's a smart-aleck teenager listening who apparently isn't interested in Joe's assassination theories and asks him, "How about a little 'Wipe Out'?"

This is the equivalent of asking a Mexican trio to play "Rancho Grande." Joe plays the dozens with him: "I wish I had my baseball bat. I'd wipe you out."

The kid gives back just as good: "I been wiped out all my life, daddy."

"If you wanna rub it in," Joe says, still drumming, "I was born wiped out. I got you."

"That's your fault, not mine," says the kid.

"Say man, hey," Joe says, looking down on him from his height. "When I don't talk back at you, that's when you should worry about it. When I talk back at you, that's when you know you are safe."

"I'm always safe," says the kid and switches the conversation. "Did you ever see a roadrunner, daddy?"

"All right, he stole the show," says Joe. "You got your problems and I got mine."

I see Joe on the Seawall about that same time, summer 1967, in front of the Murdoch Pier, where I buy a pink conch at Guyette's seashell shop. I'm six. I never forget him.

Joe is not long for Galveston by then. He makes the mistake of listening to a rich businessman who digs his music and sets up some shows for him in Acapulco, which turns into a disastrous adventure. The businessman dresses Joe up like a Voodoo doctor in flowing silk shirts, buys him good shoes with dancing taps, and a ticket to Mexico. When Joe gets there, though, his work visa and all the clothes turn out to have been bought with rubber checks. Visa-less, he ends up in Mexican prison, where he bangs on trash cans to entertain his unfortunate cellmates. The *carceleros* in charge are amused by the crazy *negrito*, though, and on weekends he's furloughed to play parties for the rich politicians and military officers. He's finally released after a few months, and surviving on pesos he busks during improvised concerts on scavenged cans he beats his way back to Galveston in early 1968.

On April 4, 1968, Martin Luther King is shot and killed while giving a speech from the balcony of the Lorraine Hotel in Memphis, Tennessee. Rioters take over parts of over 100 American cities in the following days. In San Antonio, Texas, though, they are throwing a massive party three years in the making, HemisFair 1968, a celebration commemorating the 250th anniversary of Spanish colonization of the region. The fair admits its first visitor on April 6, just two days after the assassination.

Around the same time, Joe loses his stage in Galveston when the owner of an old folks' home across from the Seawall complains he's too loud. Now the city won't let him play after 10 pm, when people don't have anywhere else to go and Joe's crowds get big. Displaced and never one to miss an opportunity to perform on a grand stage, Joe makes his way to HemisFair from Galveston, hoping to entertain the daily crowd of tens of thousands strolling through the park.

The Fair site, which includes the 500-foot Tower of the Americas with a rotating restaurant topping it, an aerial tramway, and numerous pavilions dedicated to San Antonio's heritage as a "confluence of the Americas," covers 90 acres of land bordering the southwest corner of downtown San Antonio. Before the Fair, the land is home to Polish, German, Chinese, Mexican-American, and African-American neighborhoods. It is one of the most historic sites in south Texas, with hundreds of surviving colonial structures dating back to the early 1700s. This doesn't stop the HemisFair boosters from razing the historical site. Under the guise of urban renewal, the city invokes imminent domain and evicts the residents of the 90-acre site and bulldozes over all but thirty-five of the historic structures. A reporter for the *San Antonio Express-News* celebrates this path of progress: "With the flags of many nations whipping in the breeze, San Antonians and people of the nation and world poured into what was once a haven for winos, stray dogs, and junked cars" and is now a place where "money flowed like water."

To the Fair officials, Bongo Joe must appear to be one of those former winos now displaced and disoriented: he wears Levis cut off at the knees, mismatched socks sticking out the ends of ripped sneakers, a hippie peace symbol around his neck, and a red fez atop his head decorated with Masonic symbols. Joe is rudely refused entrance to the fair grounds. He shrugs and sets up his kit on the adjoining sidewalk only to be told to leave there, too, or face the cops. "He's enough to scare an English Bulldog off a gut wagon if the bulldog didn't know him," says one observer. "He looks like an escapee from the coconut academy."

Ironically, if anyone is "a confluence of the civilizations of the Americas"—HemisFair's slogan—it's the Bahamian-descended African-American Floridian Bongo Joe. Inside the gates at the HemisFair Arena, on opening day, Ladybird Johnson gives a speech in which she hopes that the fair will "in some small way contribute to a better understanding between peoples." Joe understands he needs to move along and sets his drum barrel lengthwise and rolls it along its chines to the perimeter of the Fair.

Barred from entering the grounds, Joe can still catch glimpses of the festivities inside and hear the excited fairgoers as he heads west towards downtown and the Riverwalk.

Daddy to his daughter: "How you doing for money?"

Daughter: "Uh, I've got a dollar."

Daddy: "Well everything costs money."

A Japanese reporter asks a blond-haired blue-eyed San Antonian, "Are you Mexican or American? They told me everyone was either a Mexican or an American."

Passing Gate 2 on South Alamo Street, thirty protestors are the only reflection of the turmoil going down outside this bubble of boosterism and fake history. On one side of the street are anti-Vietnam protestors; on the other, serious-faced Mexican-American and African-American protestors. Signs read, "Our Fun is being paid for in blood." "This is not the time to celebrate." "Hemisfair is for the Rich Only." A small plane circles the Tower of the Americas trailing a banner that says "McCarthy for President." The struggling San Antonio Chapter of Dissenting Democrats of Texas can only keep the plane flying for one hour at a hundred dollars an hour fee.

Instinctively, Joe moves against the crowd and goes north on South Alamo. Two days after the fair opens, a memorial for Dr. King is held on the steps of the Alamo. A crowd of about 500—a tiny fraction of the 35,000 HemisFair-goers a few blocks away—listen to a sermon by King's personal friend, Reverend S. H. James. "We must walk as he walked," the reverend tells the crowd, "led by a distant drummer that beats out a beat of love and fellowship."

Wheeling his drums to a halt, Joe stands before the Alamo with its trademark façade, milling tourists, children dripping ice cream, and live oaks draping shade on the plaza. Joe sets up right there in front of the stone Cenotaph listing the names of the Alamo dead. Like them, he's found his final stage.

Over the next few days, tourists narrowly eye him as he tunes his drums, whistling, and sets up his sound system—three radios he's rigged together as an amplifier and a microphone he's assembled from a public phone receiver diaphragm. (Joe is hell on the payphones in the cities where he lives). He starts to whistle into his microphone, weirdly, as he plays the beat to "Tequila," "Night Train," and "When the Saints Go Marching In." But the crowd at the Alamo, Texas' holiest of holies in a state that is decidedly frontier humorless and deeply suspicious, can't initially understand his vibe. Pretty soon some stalwart citizen calls a cop over claiming Joe is disturbing the peace. Here, divine intervention occurs: the cop, apparently a more open-minded man than the HemisFair officials, gives Joe a good long listen and decides, hell, Joe isn't disturbing anyone's peace: "He's just plain good." Bennie Burns is playing guitar and harmonica on the HemisFair grounds and wanders by the Alamo and hears Joe and is impressed, too: "He's got a beat," he tells a reporter. "A beat like I've never heard."

Sam Kindrick, a *San Antonio Express-News* columnist, sees him a couple of months later playing next to the Alamo and writes, "Just three blocks from the glittering world's fair gates dwells George Coleman, a raggedy gent who whistles between his teeth and thumps everything from 'Dixie' to the 'Great Speckled Bird' on a 55-gallon oil barrel. Some might find this ridiculous, but the 20-50 persons who crowd around Coleman daily seem to find him entertaining. At any rate, they support him." He's an incongruous presence for sure, performing for the mostly white, well-fed, and margarita-ed tourists making him out in the bright, clear Hill Country light. "Nothing like this could be good, but good, God-fearing American public has just got to stop and gawk," observes Kindrick. "George Coleman couldn't be good. He couldn't be, but he was."

Joe loves playing for the crowds who wander over to the Alamo from HemisFair '68, especially the kids, whom he invites to take a turn on his barrels. On one occasion he trades his watch for a toy watch worn by a little boy who is banging away. "If your Daddy don't like the deal," he tells the boy, "You can trade back. I couldn't ever remember to wind mine and I don't really care much about time nohow." During a performance of "When the Saints Go Marching In" he stops playing abruptly and shouts at some pedestrians through his microphone, "Hey, you folks, you're running that red light." There's a wedding party across the street at the Menger Hotel and Joe plays a dissonant beat while whistling "Here Comes the Bride." The bride recognizes Joe and shouts, "Hello!" Joe responds by braying like a donkey, leaping into the air, and cackling like a chicken: "Ladies and gentlemen, the beautiful bride is a fixing to board a cab and go flying out of here—Yahoo!"

One of Joe's performances at the Alamo that year catches the attention of blues revivalist and musicologist Chris Strachwitz, president of Arhoolie Records, to this day one of the premier labels preserving Americana music.

Strachwitz is the son of Eastern European refugees whose family immigrates to America in 1947. As a teenager, he becomes obsessed with the authentic music of his adopted country—folk, rhythm and blues, bluegrass—and while living in Berkeley, California he first hears Bongo Joe on a 1959 folk and blues compilation produced for 77 Records by Houston's Mack McCormick. Two tracks feature Joe: an 8-minute improvised rendition of "This Old World is in a Terrible Condition," performed on metal drums, which is singled out by reviewers of the album as the "real revelation" on the compilation; and a recording of Joe on piano in a Galveston nightclub—the only recording of Joe on piano—that's a 2-minute staccato blues attack on the black keys that is half drumming, half keyboarding.

Years after hearing these rare field recordings, in 1968,

Strachwitz walks across a bridge in downtown San Antonio and there, to his amazement, is Joe himself playing. Between sets, he introduces himself and tells Joe of the record he's heard and asks him if he can record him. Joe politely agrees and begins to play again, but Strachwitz's portable machine craps out. Strachwitz doesn't give up. His good friend, music writer Larry Skoog, lives in town and Skoog tells Chris, "Come over to my house and we can record him there on your Magnecord machine."

Skoog's recording "studio" is a pieced-together affair in his living room. Joe heaves his drums through the suburban doorframe and sets up on a spot Strachwitz points to. "Play something, play anything," he tells him. He likes what he hears and threads a tape on a reel to reel recorder. "You're good enough for a master tape," he tells Joe. "Master what?" Joe asks. "I ain't done that in years."

Joe starts the taped session, playing only musical rhythms with none of the chatter he employs in his street act. But Strachwitz keeps saying, "Talk, talk, Joe. That's what people want." Joe complies, improvising a version of his misanthropic classic, "Innocent Little Doggie," which tells the story of how a dog will always be a better friend to you than a man; of "Transistor Radio," in which a street musician pulls a gun on a tourist, a bank teller, and a judge, demanding only their transistor radio in exchange for their life; and several more of his popular routines. The result is his only full-length recording, *George Coleman—"Bongo Joe"*. The cover photo shows Joe exultingly rattling his oil drums on the plaza in front of the Alamo; on the back are liner notes by Skoog.

The opening track, "Eloise," captures Joe's uniquely layered drum sound, a child's rattle attached to his mallets providing a rattling, rhythmic counterpoint. His off-note gap-toothed whistling slides up the scale almost out of hearing to anyone but Joe's motley collection of street dogs. The improvised story lyrics are blue: When Eloise leaves Joe and he comes sheepishly around knocking at her door, she tells him she knows it's him and to come on in. Joe hesitates but she encourages him—if you don't come on in now the Iceman will if you won't.

On "Listen at that Bull," Joe says he's broadcasting from the top of the Riverwalk's premier hotel, the Hilton. It's an instrumental track, and Joe shows off his drum skills here, hammering his sticks in a real slam fest: His drums sound like the earth's core is shifting the planet's axis. As a counterpoint to the deep rhythms, he plays the edges of the barrels, whistling an accompaniment. He can make his scavenged kit sound like a steel drum or a tympani. The hypnotizing track is punctuated by incoherent screams. "Listen at that Bull" captures Joe's real music, minus the antics. He deflates the intensity at the end, as if laughing at his own seriousness, by screaming "GRRR-eat" in the voice of Kellogg cereal's Tony the Tiger—a nod to his favorite audience members, the kids in his audience. In fact, the only audience for this recorded performance is Larry Skoog's children, sitting in the living room.

If Joe has a philosophy in life, it's revealed perhaps in "Cool It Right": there aren't two sides to a question, there's North, South, East, and West and backwards and forwards. As he tells Larry Skoog in an interview after the recording session in his living room, "Any real man, if you want to be a real man, he can't wiggle out of a situation just looking out for himself. It's impossible to improve the earth in that manner. If you can have an influence to cause people to see on a level, you can get yourself out of a situation, and you get out of a situation you don't have to worry about somebody else trying to connive or scheme a way to throw you right back in it, because you're out of it truly. You ain't out of it through scheme."

On "I Wish I Could Sing," Joe proves not only that he can sing, albeit by torturing and distorting his tonsils, but also that if he can't sing he can sure whistle with the best of birds. He also glories in having a real mic, not one of his cannibalized telephone-receiver mics, backing way off to scream his lyrics and create a sonic depth. It's what they call a *tour de force*.

"Transistor Radio" dramatizes a love of portable music players long pre-dating the boombox craze of the eighties. The narrator stalks a young woman in sixties go-go boots grooving to the sounds of her portable transistor radio. She is terrified when he pulls a .45 on her, but all he wants is her radio. A bank teller thinks the singer wants all the money in the vault, but all he wants is the teller's radio, too. When he takes his transistor radio with him to the grave, his wife tears her hair out in symbolic grief but not over him—he's taken her radio. To those who know Joe, the song reflects Joe's genius salvaging and stealing and cannibalizing electronic components and re-assembling them into microphones and speakers. It's not just about listening; it's about turning the listening components into broadcasting. But it's also a reflection of the frequent robberies that take place on the inner-city streets of San Antonio—Joe's sometimes dangerous stage.

There's the mixed-up bestiary of "Dog Eat Dog," with cats finding themselves in the doghouse; the sounds of dinosaurs going extinct on "Science Fiction." On "Crazy with Love," he's all over the drums, sounding like two drummers going at it instead of one. It's one of the tracks that makes you realize why people say Joe is not just a drummer, he plays music on the drums.

"Innocent Little Doggie" is the most popular track, albeit on very limited radio play on underground stations such as the Pacifica Station in Houston and on pirate radio stations in London in the late sixties. Joe always says he thinks he loves dogs more than people, half-humorously, but this song is no joke, a bit of musical misanthropy worthy of Mark Twain. You help out a dog, it loves you; you help out a fellow man, he stabs you in the back and steals your wife. Joe whistles the death whines of a dog in a ditch and creates a cruel beat to describe in detail the metamorphosis of the dog's rotting corpse. It's straight from the inner-city streets of San Antonio and the few who hear the song on the radio never forget it. It sounds like nothing else, the field recording of a street-corner prophet who has undeniable musical genius on a drum set-up that can't be re-created, a proto-spoken word diatribe in which you can hear the rage of riots, police-beatings, assassinations of JFK, RFK, MLK; the sixties on a street level. The song is sampled today by DJs who amplify its powerful rhythm track on nightclub dancefloors.

The entire album is performed on the spot by Joe in about the same time it takes to play the record.

The album, perhaps not coincidentally, is released on December 7th, 1968, normally a day for national mourning but subverted in the past by Pat Kirkwood to inaugurate his club openings. Joe takes his hundred-dollar payment in comped albums but never sells them; he just gives them away. The hippies who hear it think Joe is an old beatnik, but he tells them he was around way before beatniks and if anyone copied anyone, they copied him. There is even a capsule review of the album in a new counterculture rag out of San Francisco, *Rolling Stone*, which calls it "an album of vitality and mystery. Bongo Joe reveals his philosophy in deeply echoing chant, singing over the boomings of his improvised drumsticks. His monologues and dialogues depict a satirical, humorous view of modern man in plastic America."

After the recording, musicologist Larry Skoog sits down with Joe for an interview that reveals Joe's musical roots and ideas about songwriting. The songs, he says, "I make up as I go along. Got my first time yet to do the same one twice the same way." He plays the "first thing come to my mind" and changes his set up every hour in San Antonio: "Can't just rig up a set pattern like you would a bucket of water and pour it on them and expect them to drink it." He takes his cue from the improvisational jazz music of the bebop era and his taste in music leans towards the "good jazz orchestras," as Strachwitz characterizes them. Joe reels off a list of favorite jazz artists for Skoog: "Dave Brubeck, Stan Kenton, Erroll

Garner, Fats Wallace, Chick Webb, Gene Krupa, Stan Kenton, Duke Ellington, Johnny Hodges, Flip Phillips, Dizzy Gillespie."

When Skoog learns Joe is originally from Florida he asks him if he has ever been back there since leaving. Never went back to Florida, he says, and in 1968 he doesn't want to. The news media scares him with stories of civil rights disturbances going on there. That summer, Richard Nixon has been nominated for President in Miami and riots break out; three blacks are killed by gunfire. "Me, for myself, I ain't going to take part in a thing I'd rather not be around," he shakes his head.

Joe's politics will always puzzle those who take a moment to think about them. Joe doesn't bother to explain: "You don't say how good you can shine a pair of shoes," he tells Larry Skoog. "I can make them look so you can see yourself. You don't understand, and I'll exercise it. See what I mean?" In other words, trying to figure out Joe's game is an exercise in self-study. If you want to see the crazy black man HemisFair organizers saw, or a minstrel stereotype, you will see one; if you want to romanticize him as the "Magic Negro," that will reflect on you, too.

Still, in the hyperpolitical late sixties, politics is something everyone is wearing on their sleeves, or in Joe's case, on his head: on the streets, he's now wearing cut-off pants, combat boots with two different colored socks, and atop it all—a purple fez. Whether or not he's making a statement, Joe's fez—adorned with Masonic symbols, a crescent moon, and a star—can't help but summon up pictures of fez-wearing revolutionary and preacher Elijah Mohammed. In the late 1950s the cosmic jazz artist Sun Ra and his band lightheartedly adopted Elijah Mohammed's fez as part of their costume, but they quickly put the fezes away when confronted by angry Nation of Islam members at a 1957 concert in Chicago. By the late sixties, however, celebrity activists such as Mohammed Ali frequently wear the fez. Occasionally, Joe will sing about his desire to return to the Bahamas in a way that suggests an affiliation with African-American ideology of the time, but Joe is never overtly political and his antics with the crowd and with the children are disarming. To friends, Joe shrugs off politics and suggests that he feels the Middle Eastern symbols on his fez provide some kind of mystical protection to him on the streets. Like everything about Joe, his costume and the Masonic symbols on his drums are idiosyncratic, but on another level Joe's fierce independence and uniqueness are a civil rights movement all his own. Later in his life when Joe is asked about his politics he says he's probably a Republican because they believe in self-reliance.

A woman in her mid-thirties named Helen Glau first hears the be-fezed Joe on the 25th of October, 1968—she remembers the exact day twenty-seven years later in an interview. He's playing in front of the Alamo by the Cenotaph as she posts a letter in a mailbox on Alamo Street. She meets him through his dogs, which she approaches to pet. Joe is always rescuing dogs from the downtown streets and tells her he's got two big dogs at home. "I've got a list of every dog I've ever owned since I was born," he says, and later shows it to her.

She sees Joe in front of the Alamo nearly every day thereafter. It bothers her, though, that everyone is laughing and dancing and having a good time but Joe's "kitty" ends up with only twenty-six cents. He lives in a flophouse boarding room near downtown, seventeen people sharing one bathroom. One day Helen goes home and tells her mother, "Mother, we've got to help him. A man who can make people so happy ought to be doing better than that." Helen decides what Joe needs is a classified in the *San Antonio Express-News* advertising his services. She writes one up and shows it to him: "Unique entertainer, recording artist well known as 'Alamo Drummer' Avail for private parties, special engagements. Exc references."

Helen becomes Bongo Joe's unofficial manager, taking his calls and tracking him down on the streets of San Antonio for gigs and appearances. She is also one of Joe's only close friends in San Antonio. No one really asks about the exact nature of their relationship—interracial relationships are still controversial, Platonic or not—but the two are close enough to argue like an old married couple, observes one of Helen's acquaintances. Curious about this set up, a reporter calls the classified ad number and reaches Helen's mother, who tells him they are just trying to help Joe make a little money with the ad.

"You're Anglo, aren't you, and Bongo Joe is black," he says, confused.

"So what," she tells him. "Color shouldn't make a difference when you're helping someone."

When Helen first puts the ad out she hears from a lot of people who recognize Joe's talent but want to change him by putting him in a nightclub and telling him how to dress and what to sing. She tells them all, "I'm not going to change a button on Joe. When you change something, it's not authentic anymore, it's their creation not his creation." Helen understands that many of these opportunities will take away what Joe values most—his freedom, his outdoor stage, and the people on the street who love him and his music. More than one businessman shakes his head when Helen turns down a steady gig in a nightclub.

He does, however, slowly start establishing himself as part of the city's official culture, and although he doesn't play nightclubs he does accept invitations to play some high society parties around town. Sam Kindrick remembers asking the bigshots if Joe could play HemisFair in 1968 and they looked at him as if he had a piece of spinach stuck between his front teeth. In September of 1970, though, there's Joe playing at the San Antonio Art League Jamboree held at the home of Marshall Steves—HemisFair 1968's President. Steves, whose ancestors from the Canary Islands arrived in San Antonio in 1731, is San Antonio royalty living in a splendid new home. The high modernist architect O'Neil Ford (designer of HemisFair's Tower of the

Americas) departs from his usual aesthetic and has created for the Steveses a Spanish colonial hacienda, completed in 1964 and located north of downtown San Antonio. Under the direction of the Steveses, who collect Mexican arts and crafts, Ford unashamedly scavenges seventeenth-century arches, winding stone stairs, iron grilles, and domed tile ceilings from San Miguel de Allende in Mexico. The three outdoor courtyards are perfect for social events.

Joe is singing "Night Train" and drumming in one of these outdoor courtyards, where arts patrons sip tequila, when he spots a baby grand piano in the main living room of the Steves house. It is a high-ceilinged space with thick white walls decorated in Mexican curios ("junk" sniffs the refined Ford when he sees it hanging on "his" walls) and framed by three ancient arches transported from San Miguel. Joe crosses the Saltillo-tiled floors, sits down on the piano bench, and begins to play. Sam Kindrick, covering the high-society fundraiser for the *San Antonio Express-News*, is shocked by what he hears: Joe can play the hell out of a piano, drumming the piano stool with one hand while he punches out a Fats Domino song with the other. He moves from rock to jazz to classical, jumping up and down from the stool, making bird calls and other wild sonic mimicry.

"Where in the devil did you learn to play a piano like that," he asks Joe, who continues fingering the keys.

"In that old Florida orphans home I came from."

"Do you read music?"

"Never saw no need for it."

The highbrows at the Steves house spread the word of Joe's amazing piano performance and two local promoters try to book Joe in their clubs playing piano. But again, Joe turns them down, preferring the streets of San Antonio where every day is a new experience.

Not long after playing the high society party, Joe is playing the nearly deserted downtown streets on a winter night—trying to make enough money to get something to eat—when a man he knows walks up to him and asks,

Did Beatniks Kill John F. Kennedy?

"Joe, how long are you going to be here? Stay right here, I want you to meet someone." Joe stays put, the wind cold and blowing hard. He's rigged a scavenged motor to his three-wheeled bike and runs the engine to keep himself warm, holding his hands up to the manifold. After a couple of hours, a large man in a full-length coat comes around the corner of the cold empty streets with two girls on his arm. It's Muhammed Ali. Ali and the girls hang around and listen to Joe for almost an hour in the cold, and Ali keeps telling Joe, "Man, you're good. You ought to be playing in a nightclub," but Joe just shakes his head. When Ali leaves, he gives Joe a bear hug and a fifty-dollar bill. Joe later says, "When he hugged me, he like to squeeze the shit out of me!"

In 1971, after three years of playing to the national and international crowds visiting San Antonio, Joe's talent is impressive enough for him to be invited to perform at the New Orleans Jazz and Heritage Festival—probably by a Festival official who has taken in his show in front of the Alamo. Joe doesn't think anyone in San Antonio will believe he's been invited to the prestigious gig so he sends Sam Kindrick a copy of his contract with the festival organizers. He'll play there nine times, most famously one year when he sits in on piano for his idol, Dizzy Gillespie. On Bourbon Street, Joe and Dizzy play an impromptu concert, Dizzy Gillespie stroking George's oil can drums, George on a portable keyboard.

On December 1st, 1973, Helen Glau and friends throw a birthday party for Joe, his 50th. They screen San Antonio filmmaker George Nelson's short documentary film, "Bongo Joe." Nelson's film has already won a Silver Award at the International TV and Film Festival New York. In the film, Joe looks part Salvation Army, part Jimi Hendrix, wearing Bermuda shorts with army boots, a long-sleeved shirt with ruffled collar and cuffs, a necklace chain with a gold medallion, and his maroon fez. A button on his collar reads, "Kiss me, I'm Jewish." Nelson follows Joe around for several weeks to assemble the film. Joe is 6'3" and 260 pounds, and he puts it all into pounding the drums for the film crew at concerts in front of the Alamo, on Villita Street, and in an east-side cemetery—which Joe calls "poor people's park." Much of the footage focuses on Joe interacting with children, who take a turn on the big drums.

After filming, Joe sometimes goes to eat at a diner on east Houston St. near the tracks. Nelson tries to interview him on tape, but Joe's deep, gravelly, and mumbled voice is hard to make out. Perhaps, thinks Nelson, this is why Joe prefers to whistle rather than sing while performing, and why he sings a song called "I Wish I Could Sing."

While Joe finds his place in San Antonio and settles down there to live life on his own terms, the Cellar, back in Fort Worth, is killed by its own success. By the early 1970s many clubs around the state and country have imitated its live rock format, and waitresses in underwear are no longer a novelty: strip clubs, some featuring full nudity, are now legal and ubiquitous. And when the drinking age is rolled back to 18 in 1972 kids don't have to sneak into bars anymore and lie about their age. However, the most crucial way the times change, relegating the Cellar to another era, is Kennedy's legacy—the civil rights acts of the 1960s. In San Antonio the major clientele of the Cellar had been members of an integrated armed forces stationed on five bases around the city, and the San Antonio Cellar shuttered in 1962 in part because no blacks were allowed in the club. In Houston in the late sixties, young blacks drive by the whites-only Houston Cellar and blast shotguns at the club's entrance. Joe Ely, the singer for a band called The Neurotic Sheep, quits his singing gig at the Houston Cellar when the management won't let his black friends come see him perform. The Fort Worth Cellar manages to stay open operating under these Jim Crow conditions until 1972; the Dallas Cellar folds in 1973.

The end of the flagship Cellar in Fort Worth begins when four black TCU students are denied admission to the club in the spring of 1972. Fort Worth's Human Relations Committee files a complaint against Kirkwood, citing the city's "open accommodations ordinance," one which has never been tested in court. Kirkwood, in typical fashion, asks Judge Harold Valderas to re-schedule the hearing until after deer-hunting season is over. Valderas humorlessly denies the request. At trial in early December, Kirkwood pleads no contest and is fined two hundred and fifty dollars. Valderas calls Kirkwood's no-blacks policy "a slap in the face for local citizens." Kirkwood doesn't learn his lesson—few have taught him one—and says he'll shut the Cellar down rather than change his admissions policy.

"I'm going to run my place the way I see fit," he says. "If anyone doesn't like it, let him sue me. I'll probably double my business. If I don't like the way somebody looks or smells, he don't get in. I don't care if he's red, yellow, black, or green."

Specifically banned are "dopers, homosexuals, and cops."

But Kirkwood's moment is over. His equal discrimination against everyone argument sounds like Archie Bunker, but no one's laughing. On August 19th, 1972, the Cellar closes with little commotion. Fort Worth Police Chief T. S. Walls condemns the place as having been "a center of ultraliberal activities." Almost wistfully, however, a plainclothes cop says, "It just seems like they are the pioneers of the sexual revolution. The Cellar was the first of its kind . . . now X-rated movies and such leave nothing to the imagination." No mention of the city's enforcement of open access laws is made in the Cellar's obituary. Kirkwood says he has closed the club because it is structurally deteriorating and because downtown has gone totally dead after dark: all the nightlife has moved to Camp Bowie Road on the West side of town.

While the stages at the Cellars go dark, Joe's stage grows, as if he had the right idea all the time by avoiding the segregated nightclubs and playing the one place where he is free, fully, to be himself—the streets. By the mid-1970s, there is a growing recognition in Texas of street and folk musicians such as Joe. UT Austin has a thriving folklore program under Brownsville, Texas native Américo Paredes, who first writes about Mexican street musicians in *The Brownsville Herald* in 1936 when he's only eighteen years old. As a professor of folklore in the 1960s, Paredes, along with Roger Abrahams, mentors white boys such as Pat Mullen, Tary Owens, and Glen Alyn who are all fascinated by black blues musicians. Following this trend, in 1976 Joe is a featured performer at the inaugural Texas Folklife Festival. His drums are spray-painted in DayGlo pink and green, and Joe wears his fez or a combat helmet, a yellow jacket, and red knickers: the pictures of him playing are suddenly in color, as if the world has changed from black and white. A piano is put in front of him and, yes, he plays only the black keys, F#.

In April, 1976, Joe performs for his second President of the United States when he is picked up by Gerald Ford's re-election committee for a 12-city Texas tour. "We don't have anything like that in Washington," Ford's campaign manager, Ron Nessen, says as he watches a performance by Joe. "Maybe we should." Ford is behind Reagan in the Texas polls. Helen Glau says "George never played so well before, until Mr. Ford shook his hand and said a few words to him."

After the Kennedy assassination, Gerald Ford, then a young Representative from Michigan, was an unlikely member of the Warren Commission; he primarily served as a mole for J. Edgar Hoover. By the mid-1970s, when Ford is a one-term President, the Warren Commission report is increasingly suspect in post-Watergate America. One of the skeptics is a renegade young Latino reporter named Geraldo Rivera who obtains a pirated copy of the famous Zapruder film and screens it on the national TV show "Good Night, America" on March 6th, 1975. It is the first time the public sees the gory footage, although copies of the film have been circulated underground for many years. "You might not want your kids to be watching," Rivera warns in promotional spots, so of course hordes of teens and pre-teens do. A few years later they are forming punk rock bands with names like "The Dead Kennedys." When the headshot occurs in the screening, Rivera says, "That's the most horrifying thing I've ever seen. That's the most upsetting thing I've ever seen."

Panelists on the program, including political commentator and comedian Dick Gregory, point out that close-up frames of the film show Kennedy's head clearly being thrown back by the kill shot, whereas the Warren Commission Report claims Kennedy is shot from behind, by Oswald. Belief in the single-shooter theory has already been eroded by a decade of conspiracy literature, beginning in 1966 with the bestselling *Rush to Judgment*. Public skepticism leads to the establishment of the House Select Committee on Assassinations in 1976. The authors of the committee's report, chaired by Henry Gonzalez of Texas, conclude that there is "a high probability that two gunmen fired at President John F. Kennedy." Oswald's Dallas friend George de Mohrenschildt contributes a 200-page memoir about Oswald to the report in which he argues, based on his numerous conversations with Oswald, that Oswald was an admirer of the President and had no motive for trying to kill him. He even maintains, "Maybe, had he [Oswald] lived longer, he would have fitted better into the scheme of American life, he would have joined the group of love-children, would have grown a beard and certainly would have been among the protestors against the war in Vietnam."

The HSCA report demonstrates what is already obvious: after 13 years of conspiracy theories about the assassination, Kennedy's official life and achievements are overshadowed by the circumstances of his death—that, and the rumors surfacing about his subterranean life involving numerous mistresses.

Joe's career arc is the opposite. After years of obscurity, he is now officially a legend and a fixture on the streets of San Antonio. Tourists hear about him before they come to the city and seek out his performances.

A typical evening in the 1970s: Joe turns on his PA and

begins gathering a crowd. A policeman walks by and calls out "Hi Joe, how's everything?" and waves and smiles. Ambulance drivers, tow truck drivers, and street cleaners all wave or say hello. "Five minutes to show time, everybody," Joe announces on "Happy Corner, USA," Joe's name for his stage. He loves children and tells the curious: "This is the real reason I do it." Joe just keeps getting better and better. One of his tricks: he tapes his performances on a portable cassette player and plays them back after hours while sipping on a soda in his rented room, listening for what gets the biggest applause and thinking how he can improve on it.

San Antonio in the mid-seventies is now one of the most popular tourist destinations in the country, with the sprawling Hemisphere complex, the Riverwalk (a San Antonio River flood control project turned into a Cypress-shaded, restaurant- and bar-lined entertainment district), and, in the middle of it all, the remains of an 18th-century Spanish mission augmented by the iconic limestone façade in the 1850s—Texas's monument to colonization, the Alamo. And right in front of it is Bongo Joe. It is likely that many people remember Bongo Joe performing long after they've forgotten the specifics of the fates of the Alamo defenders.

Future poet and first Mexican-American Rhodes Scholar recipient, John Phillip Santos, is driven by his parents many a night to hear Joe's performances in front of the Alamo during the 1970s. The rattles on Joe's mallets as they hit his DayGlo pink oil drums sound to him as if they contain the teeth of defeated conquerors. Joe sings about his girlfriends, his dogs, his hard-life experiences, his travels, but sometimes he just laughs, crazily, as he finds a new beat. Young Santos finds Joe's performances to be revelatory: if Joe can do this in downtown San Antonio in front of the Alamo, soliciting change for his wheelbarrow "kitty," then anyone anywhere can make music and poetry from the life around them. Sometimes he sees Joe walking the streets of San Antonio when he isn't performing, two or three dogs roped to his drum cart and wearing a harsh look on his face, a world-weary look, one that disappears when he is playing his drums for the crowds.

The dangerous downtown streets can wipe the smile right off a man's face, but Joe has a persona that keeps both himself and his listeners safe. In 1978, Joe witnesses a man wield a knife while robbing the Kress Drug Store across from the Alamo. The robber steals eight dollars-worth of costume jewelry. Joe tricks him into riding with him on his motorized bicycle and in a low-speed getaway delivers him to a coffee shop on 4th and Broadway, where the cops are waiting. He foils many a hijacking by distracting people and keeps a lot of people from getting their ass whupped over the years—Joe knows how to handle a crowd, a skill he honed in the rowdy, crowded Cellar.

But conditions deteriorate downtown in the early '80s. His kitty is robbed three times in one year. Joe doesn't want to need anyone's protection, and after he's robbed for the fourth time he purchases a .45. In 1982 a drunken tourist named Manuel Rubio shouts racial slurs and threatens him as he's playing for a crowd of about thirty tourists. Rubio struts around, pulling down his pants, and is falling all over the tourists when Joe sees him go for what he thinks is a gun in his back pocket that turns out to be a knife. Joe pulls his .45 and shoots him. He doesn't like to talk about it, doesn't really remember later what happens. He just knows if he hadn't shot, the guy would have cut him. Joe has a lot of fans who are influential in the city and he gets a five-year probated sentence.

After the shooting incident, however, the police seem to keep their distance from Joe. Thugs wait until the end of his performance and rob him of the day's take. Finally, he has to give up his days performing on the Alamo site and move to a safer location. In his absence, Joe tells friends, he's noticed the crime rate has gone way up around the Alamo shrine, and he attributes this to his leaving: Joe has always been there to diffuse situations.

Joe moves his stage to a landing next to the Commerce

Street Bridge and near the Hilton Hotel, a couple of blocks from the Alamo. The bridge is on a busy traffic rotary, and Joe has to compete with the noises of the automobiles and buses. As he plays, the cars circle the empty traffic island, the site, locals say, where the survivors of the Alamo siege were executed by the Mexican army. The original American bohemian poet, Walt Whitman, memorializes where they fell in one of his wild songs:

> *The second Sunday morning they were brought out in squads, and massacred ... it was*
> *beautiful early summer;*
> *The work commenced about five o'clock and was over by eight.*
> *None obeyed the command to kneel,*
> *Some made a mad and helpless rush ... some stood stark and straight,*
> *A few fell at once, shot in the temple or heart ... the living and dead lay together,*
> *The maimed and mangled dug in the dirt ... the newcomers saw them there;*
> *Some half-killed attempted to crawl away,*
> *These were despatched with bayonets, or battered with the blunts of muskets;*
> *A youth not seventeen years old seized his assassin till two more came to release him,*
> *The three were all torn, and covered with the boy's blood.*
> *At eleven o'clock began the burning of the bodies;*
> *And that is the tale of the murder of the four hundred and twelve young men,*
> *And that was a jetblack sunrise.*

San Antonio in the 1970s is a much-conflicted place with the Alamo and this unmarked massacre site at its center, a still-colonized city that is 50% Mexican-American in population but annually celebrates a huge "Fiesta" in honor of Mexico's loss of the Texas territories during the Texas Revolution of 1836. (Walt Whitman's contemporary, Henry David Thoreau, went to jail rather than pay taxes supporting the ensuing Mexican-American War of 1846-1848). San Antonio's major tourist attraction is a graveyard, essentially. Joe's music from the Commerce Street Bridge draws people to this site; they alter their pace as they walk toward the drums, stepping in time, curious about the wailing musical ruckus by Conrad Hilton's Hotel. It's hard at this point to imagine San Antonio without Bongo Joe. What he brings to the streets of San Antonio is a much-needed sense of fun and of life and celebration, something more than just a trip to the mausoleum-like Alamo, where wearing a hat or cap inside earns you a steep fine for disrespect. In performance during this time, Joe is reportedly like a whirling Dervish on his drums, an intense man on a mission with a message, nothing like other street performers scratching out barely recognizable covers of popular music on out-of-tune instruments. He's an unexpected good time, and you can't help but smile at him, people say. Behind it all, though, they sense his real talent and originality and a bit of an edge as well, if they are not always sure how that edge is lightly cutting them. Fans from all over the world sign the cylinder of his oil-barrel drums and inscribe messages such as "Bongo Joe, You are Forever."

In the mid-eighties, Johnny Carroll and Arvel Stricklin are playing at a San Antonio hotel and make a special trip across town to put a few bills in Joe's tip jar. They spot him performing by the Commerce Street Bridge, roll down their window, and call out to their fellow Cellar Dweller. Arvel tells Joe he is looking good, and for a moment in the sunlight they are happy to see each other out of the darkness that was the Cellar. Then they drive on and leave Joe to his own concert in the streets.

In 1988, the twenty-fifth anniversary of Kennedy's death, investigative reporter Jack Anderson hosts a primetime TV special on the assassination. The exposé includes an interview with Pat Kirkwood and a cheesy re-enactment of the Secret Service party that night. An out of tune barroom piano plays but isn't seen (is that Cannibal Jones on the black keys?) as women in bikinis gyrate in front of the suits. "Who's guarding the President?" an actor portraying Kirkwood asks. A drunken agent says, "Don't ask me—everybody's here." Kirkwood's actual voice says, "They showed up about one o'clock and proceeded to have an awful lot of fun." The re-enactment shows a woman sitting on an agent's lap and undoing her top for him, showing her breasts. "They partied with some of Jack Ruby's strippers, who joined in the festivities. As the party heated up, so did tempers," narrates Anderson, as two drunken agents start brawling. They knock into a Cellar waitress, who spills her drinks. Unfortunately, Cannibal Jones does not sweep in to clean up the mess with his V-room broom. "It begins to break up about five, five-thirty. Everyone was just having too much fun," Kirkwood says on camera. His hair and beard are now grey, but he's still looking trim and wearing a black shirt and gray coat, leaning back in a chair and clearly enjoying telling the story. Later, off camera, he tells Anderson, "The agents were shit-faced. They were drinking pure Everclear."

Oliver Stone's film *JFK* follows in 1991 and Kennedy is killed again and again in a forty-five-minute trial scene conducted by New Orleans DA Jim Garrison in which the Zapruder film is the main evidence. Garrison is played by Kevin Costner, who disturbingly resembles the real-life Lee Harvey Oswald. Joe Pesci plays a lowlife conspirator named David Ferrie and has the best line in the movie. The president's death, he says, is a "mystery wrapped in a riddle inside an enigma." The president's death has taken on a life of its own and is now the locus of endless story-making.

None of the locations of the original Cellars exist at that point. Fort Worth builds a huge convention center that squats like a giant flying saucer in the city's old center. Somewhere in the bowels of the convention center is preserved the stage at the Tenth and Main location of the Cellar, quite by accident of construction. No one is interested in memorializing this stage with a plaque or anything else. Fort Worth seems happy to forget that part of its past and keeps its frontier heritage carefully corralled in the tourist-friendly Stock Yards entertainment complex.

Late one night in the 1990s, a few years before his death, Pat Kirkwood walks the deserted downtown streets of Fort Worth near where the old Cellars used to be. He pulls out a pistol and fires it in the air and patiently waits for the police to show up, for anyone to notice. The streets echo the gunfire, lifeless. He puts his gun back in his pocket and walks on. He's made his point.

Not long after, Kirkwood, now a real estate agent, puts the legendary Four Deuces up for sale—but with a catch he describes in a classified ad in the real estate section. "Double or Nothing" is the heading: "OK high rollers, let's agree to a price and flip double or nothing for the Four Deuces at 2222 Jacksboro Hwy. 3 historical acres. Flexible for fast deal! Call Pat Kirkwood." No one takes him up on the offer. Probably because they know they will lose.

In 1990, Michael Mehl and Steve Henry, editors of the alt-pub *San Antonio Current*, create a San Antonio arts program for public TV station KLRN called "Almost Live from the Liberty Bar." The short-lived show features outside-the-mainstream artists and personalities and opens with Joe performing "Cool It Right" in front of the Liberty Bar. The soundtrack combines the Arhoolie track with additional music by Joe, who plays a beat-up Yamaha keyboard given to him by Helen Glau that is programmed with a blues-organ setting. Joe embodies everything the show hopes to represent—he's iconoclastic, independent, off-kilter, edgy, and unconventional, says Mehl. The show is indeed all those things, starts to gain an audience, and is therefore promptly cancelled after a few episodes.

One of the show's producers, Steve Henry, later arranges for Joe to receive a Lifetime Achievement award (made up just for Joe) at the *Current*-sponsored San Antonio Music

Awards, held in a downtown nightclub. Francois Huybrecht, conductor of the San Antonio Symphony Orchestra, gets on stage and takes a turn on Joe's drums. After the show, the *Current* interviews Joe. Joe dislikes interviews, which he says are like dates: "You think of all the things you are going to talk about, and when the time comes, you don't know what to say."

"I like dogs, sometimes better than people," he admits.

He's still doing after-hour gigs in the city in the early nineties, mostly impromptu parties he's invited to. Sometimes he plays the clarinet instead of drums or piano. For years he's annually played a Greek party during the spring semester at UT Austin, but he's in poor health in 1991 and has to leave the gig early. This leads to rumors of his death. A premature obituary even runs in the *Austin Chronicle*.

The last interview with Joe is conducted in 1995 by Pat Mullen, who hasn't seen Joe since he interviewed him on the Seawall in 1967. Pat is now a folklore professor at Ohio State and writes a brilliantly self-conscious study of white scholars who have devoted their careers to studying the life and work of black folk musicians called *The Man Who Adores the Negro*. It includes a chapter on Bongo Joe. In 1995, he finds Joe in the Audie Murphy Memorial Hospital in San Antonio: Joe is suffering from diabetes and kidney disease. It's a sunny day and they sit on the outdoor patio of the hospital, Joe in a wheelchair. One of the visitors has brought a little dog and it catches Joe's attention throughout the interview, Joe punctuating his answers with his signature bark heard over the years in his performances: "Arsh-arsh!"

Pat starts the interview by remarking, "I heard that down in Galveston thirty years ago you were ahead of your time fifty years, now I'm starting to believe it." Bebop has led to beatnik to hippies to rap. Now fans begin to see Joe as an originator of rap. "I rap," says Joe, "but not that bullshit they're putting down now. I play fundamental beat music."

He tells Pat he's played on the streets up until about six years ago. "Played most of the days of the week—never got too cold, never got too hot. It didn't get too cold, not to me, 'cause I was having fun."

"What did people like the best in your show, Joe?" Mullen asks.

"Playing and shaking it around, once in a while I'd kick my foot up. Showmanship."

Joe has put on a smile through four decades of living in the segregated south, but now in his old age, he gives a glimpse into the double-consciousness that required: "Nobody ever took my clowning the wrong way. The grand-dragon ought to see me now. They wouldn't pay it no mind. I knew their reaction better than they knew their own."

Helen Glau is present throughout the interview and she has brought Joe's personal papers with her to answer a few of the hospital administrators' questions. There are pictures of Joe at the Texas Folklife Festival and one ancient, folded glossy of him in top hat and tails from his days performing in the Officer's Clubs during WWII. Joe has no family other than Helen and her brother. He has been living with them near downtown for years, after the city condemned the boarding house he lived in until the early 1980s.

At the end of the interview, Mullen puts his tape recorder in his pocket and pushes Joe's wheelchair into the cafeteria where lunch is being served. On the tape you can hear the muffled sounds of the wheelchair rolling, muted conversation. Then the chair stops, and Joes says, clearly, "Come on back this afternoon. There's something really important I need to tell you . . ."

Joe dies in December of 1999. Helen and others collect tributes for an obituary in the *San Antonio Express-News*. Michael Mehl says of Joe, "He was the pre-eminent performance artist. What strikes me as his legacy is how fiercely independent, how iconoclastic he was." Quint Davis, producer of the New Orleans Jazz and Heritage Festival, says "He was a real talent. He wasn't just a curiosity." Helen Glau knows him best: "We were friends for 31 years and I helped him set up his performances, but he once told me that no one would ever come between him and his people. He said as long as there were people out there to listen, he would be there. He would turn down a better-paying gig to go to play to people on the street." Joe played with Sammy Davis, Jr. and Dizzy Gillespie, she says, and many famous people heard him on the streets of San Antonio. On the eve of the Kennedy Assassination, Helen says in the newspaper story, Joe played for the President. Joe's body is cremated, Helen safekeeping his ashes.

San Antonians do pay tribute to Joe in the years after his death, but it's a city less interested in promoting its African-American heritage than its Hispanic heritage. Even local African-American artists concentrate more on preserving the legacy of "high-brow" rather than "low-brow" artists such as Joe. Not long after Joe's passing, though, San Antonio artist Kathleen Trenchard and other fans of Joe lobby the city's Public Art Department to fund a statue of him near the Commerce Street bridge. Originally from New Orleans, Trenchard hears in Joe's call and response style of music an echo of New Orleans second line dance music. But the Public Arts Department turns down her proposal to create a memorial to Joe—they are interested only in new, not "historic" art installations. Trenchard and local architect Jon Thompson go it on their own, and create Dia De Los Muertos altars to Joe in 2000 and 2001. The altars are set up at the intersection of E. Commerce and Losoya Street and include pictures from Helen Glau's files and a cut paper wall hanging, a luminaria, created by Trenchard and depicting Joe playing his drums and wearing his classic fez. For the 2001 altar, George Nelson's documentary on Joe runs on a small battery-powered TV. It's street art for a street artist.

Trenchard's exhibit inspires a similar and larger scale one at San Antonio's Institute of Texan Cultures, a Dia De Los Muertos altar for him that opens to the public on October 31st, 2002. The exhibit, coordinated by Helen Glau, includes his last set of oil-barrel drums, the motorized scooter he carted them on, his handwritten list of all the dogs he owned, and his collection of tobacco pipes. "Get Well" cards from all over the world are tacked to a wall. Helen is often an unofficial docent for the exhibit during its three-year run. She likes to laugh and point to the eight-year-premature obituary run by *The Austin Chronicle*, a part of the exhibit. Perhaps the most remarkable item in the exhibit: one of Joe's pipes, its bowl shaped in the form of John F. Kennedy's head. When Joe puffed on it, Kennedy's head, severed at the hairline, must have glowed read and curled smoke.

From 2006 to 2009 the Beat Generation officially becomes antique with the fiftieth anniversary of the publications of "Howl" (1956), *On the Road* (1957), and *Naked Lunch* (1959). Beat Generation symposia and readings occur in New York, Chicago, Paris, and London. But you still can't read Allen Ginsberg's "Howl" in its entirety on the public airwaves in America in 2006—too many banned words—and teaching *Naked Lunch*, even in a university, can get you fired. *Naked Lunch*'s author, William S. Burroughs, once presciently pointed out that the long-term effect of Jack Kerouac's "Beat Generation" was the opening of a thousand coffee shops in America. He's right. In America, the coffee shop has become the safe space for renegade poetry readings, jazz concerts, nouveau folk music, art openings, stand-up comedy, and any number of happenings. But there is never another "coffee house" like the Cellar, and there never will be.

In 2013, Dallas plans a tightly-controlled official memorial program marking the fiftieth anniversary of the Kennedy Assassination. Streets around Dealey Plaza are closed and barricaded. There's a lottery held for admission tickets to the thirty-four-minute ceremony and the winners have to go through a background check and security screening. A couple of blocks east of Dealey Plaza the un-anointed hold up signs saying Kennedy was killed by the CIA and by LBJ. One man yells incongruously at onlookers, "There's no law that says you have to pay taxes." Conspiracy theorist and radio entertainer Alex Jones holds a protest march and his supporters are pushed back by Dallas County sheriff deputies.

Overall, it's an underwhelming memorial moment. *Texas Monthly* doesn't even mark the fiftieth with a cover story, as they had done the less numerically significant thirty-fifth anniversary of the assassination: Instead, a story on oil and gas fracking is featured. Inside the November 1993 issue, though, memorialists remind us that it was Democrats, not Republicans, who fought against civil rights in Texas. Dallas is remembered as a highly cultured, cosmopolitan place in 1963, and Oswald as an outsider. In one of the few moments of genuine insight in the issue, Texas historian Don Graham points out that 1400 books have been written about the assassination, a "cottage industry" that has gotten us nowhere closer to the truth and ultimately reveals more about the men—and they are all men—who have written the books than the events of those day. And Oswald has stolen the show—it's all about him, not Kennedy.

Across the country in Los Angeles, California, in front of the Nokia Theater, there's another moment on November 22nd that captures the muted fiftieth anniversary. At a press junket for the upcoming American Music Awards, two young women reporters are discussing what Miley Cyrus should wear to the show because "she can be really beautiful." It's only been a few months since her infamous "twerking" dance with Robin Thicke at the MTV awards. The junket is being held in a large white tent, and through the entrance flaps comes a longhaired man in sunglasses, carrying a guitar.

One of the reporters goes *sotto voce*: "FYI, Miley Cyrus's father is over there strumming a guitar. Billy Ray Cyrus."

"Let's ask him what she's going to wear," a colleague whispers. "I want his daughter to look beautiful."

At that moment, Cyrus puts down his guitar and whistles, trying to attract the attention of the tent-full of reporters. "Hey ever'body," he gestures. "If we could have a moment of silence for President John F. Kennedy, if that's all right with you all? Is that OK? Ever'body for just a moment just think of JFK. One moment of silence please."

He sits down in a folding chair, his guitar in his lap. The level of chatter in the tent continues—no one is paying any attention to him. It's an awkward moment. The two reporters worried about Miley's wardrobe choices put their hands over their mouths in order not to laugh into their microphones.

Cyrus begins glumly strumming on his guitar.

"Well, I mean this is the fiftieth anniversary," says one of the young women.

"Really, in a tent?" says her co-host.

Their producer chimes in, "Yeah, you were talking the whole way through this."

Serendipitously, but years in the making, a documentary about the Cellar titled "You Must Be Weird or You Wouldn't Be Here" premieres at the recently restored Ridglea Theater on Camp Bowie Road on November 22nd, 2013. Filmmaker Jim McCrary and his wife have spent four years interviewing surviving Cellar Dwellers. The film also features an interview with an avuncular Bob Schieffer, who provides an historical perspective on Fort Worth's frontier origins and an account of the night he ushered the secret service to the Cellar. He's still not sure, he says smiling, what the agents might or might not have been drinking that night. The film shows the good and the bad side of the Cellar, including its No Blacks policy. One viewer later posts on Facebook, "What color was Cannibal Jones?" Another jokes that he saw a couple of Secret Service agents lurking around at the film's premiere. There's a musical jam afterwards, featuring Arvel Stricklin, Jr. and a dozen other former Cellar musicians.

The Cellar documentary, premiered during the fiftieth-anniversary commemoration of the assassination, turns out to be far more representative of the moment than Dallas's re-writing of history, *Texas Monthly*'s downplaying of it, or even Billy Ray Cyrus's strummed attempt at a tribute to Kennedy. The Kennedy Assassination is only one brief moment in the Cellar's history and not the most important one—those important moments are musical milestones, such as the future members of ZZ Topp first performing there, and early performances by Johnny Nash, Joe Ely, and comedian George Carlin.

In the fifty years since the assassination, the very idea of history has changed, in large part because of Kennedy's death and the increasing public skepticism about the government's version of events on November 22, 1963. By 2013, Americans are used to believing that our government lies to us, and the whole idea of history as "the truth" is an unsupportable one. It is replaced by the concept of postmodern history, in which the focus is not so much on finding the truth as it is in telling stories about the supposed truth, stories that frequently focus on previously marginalized actors. That is, not on Kennedy, but characters such as Bongo Joe. In a post-modern era, we don't need another book on the Kennedy assassination, but we do need a book on Bongo Joe.

As Joe sings, there aren't two sides to question: there's north, south, east, west, plus backwards and forwards.

Eighty-four years ago (as of 2017) Bongo Joe's friend Sammy Davis, Jr., at the age of 7, starred in a 1933 all black short musical subject called "Rufus Jones for President." It tells the story of a mother's dream that someday her son will grow up to be President of the United States. The film is of course Depression-era, Jim Crowe musical fantasy, with Sammy tap-dancing and singing precociously in an ersatz Oval Office. Eight decades later, a black man has served two terms as president. The stories of black men such as Abraham Bolden, whom Kennedy termed the Jackie Robinson of the Secret Service, or the story of the black waiter who brought Kennedy his breakfast on November 22nd and nervously asked for a memento to remember the occasion by—these stories exist in a different era than today, when it could well be a white waiter asking President Obama for a similar memento. Maybe that's why Joe disassembled that piano at the Cellar in 1964—the year Congress passed the Civil

Rights Act—and walked out of a club that would not allow blacks admission well into the 1970s.

The story of Bongo Joe playing for Kennedy the last night of his life is apocryphal, known only to a few. But Joe did tell the story, according to a close friend, and he was never known to make up stories. The story seems true particularly because of some of the details—for example, "Mrs. Kennedy was not there." On one level, it is like all stories about the Kennedy assassination—it's just a story. But it's a good story, if you're Kennedy. If his legacy is his civil rights agenda, it's fitting he reportedly spent his last night relaxing listening to a black street performer. Joe, a humble man by all accounts, in many ways a "regular guy" as people described him to me, would never have thought in terms of a leaving a "legacy." For Joe, a friend of his told me, playing for Kennedy was the proudest moment of his life.

Today, city regulations make it nearly impossible for street performers such as Joe to make a living. A bagpipe player occasionally performs on Commerce Street, where Joe performed. There are many more evangelic groups holding forth on the downtown streets than actual street performers. The last time I visited, in 2017, even the bagpipe player was gone. But as I sat just below the Commerce Street Bridge at La Paloma restaurant, I heard the sounds of a drum solo. At street level, on a corner near the traffic circle—just across the street from where Bongo Joe used to play—is a young black man with an eight-piece professional drum set, gleaming in the sunlight. He's technically precise and makes impressive runs across the array of drums. I don't see a "kitty" nearby and wonder how he makes money. When he stops for a break, I ask him if he knows who Bongo Joe is. He doesn't. A man about my age who is my parking attendant remembers Joe, though, and smiles when I ask about him.

George Coleman's *This is Bongo Joe* is currently available as a CD issued by Arhoolie Records. Nine tracks from the original album can be heard gratis on YouTube.

In the past two years, the number of views have increased from the hundreds into the thousands. Random DJs around the world are starting to sample Joe's unique drum styles and patterns and his bebop improvised lyrics and raps. Joe is seen as everything from a "Beat" poet to a forerunner of rap and spoken word.

In 2014, the Poet Laureate of San Antonio, Carmen Tafolla, included a poem about Bongo Joe in *This River Here: Poems of San Antonio*. She gets it right as an epitaph, capturing the difficulties of Joe's life belied by his ever-present smile, the miracle of creating joyful music out of that life, and references not the Kennedy but the Martin Luther King assassination.

> *Yeah, we know he's been long dead. Maybe ten,*
> *Or twenty years, but we who heard 'im Know*
> *See and Hear and Feel it in our bones*
> *Clang clang, ting ting, tingalong tingding*
> *Holding up a smile, pouring through the tough patch*
> *Hurting, sad or worried, whistling all the while*
> *Hope stirred by a gentle King, assassination only*
> *Caused him to sing padda rappatap, bang bong bing.*

Joe wrote his own epitaph, though, many years before as a young man in his mid-thirties, standing on a downtown street corner in Houston in 1957 and recorded by Mack McCormack. The recording has a grainy, tinny, gramophone sound to it. George sounds older than he would twenty years later. It's a diasporic blues riff in the middle of "This Old World is in a Terrible Condition" in which the mask he puts on to perform is briefly removed.

> *I want to go back to Nassau*
> *When I die*
> *I don't want to go to heaven when I die*
> *Amen*

Did Beatniks Kill John F. Kennedy?

That is why I seek to find
Another planet
To rest upon
Due to my foreign accent
I wouldn't know how to say 'that'
I'm forced to say 'dat'
Dat is my heritage
Cause this old world, the planet earth
Is in a terrible condition

And Bongo Joe rattles his kitty.

Rob Johnson
1 September 2017
heard Joe age six 1967
Guyette Gift Shop, Galveston Seawall

Photo courtesy of Jon Thompson

Stories about Joe appear on message boards by fans who saw him perform. As is true for me, they never forgot him. No one has a bad word to say against him. In fact, he's faring a good deal better these days than the dead Kennedys.

Found on line at message boards:

George Coleman (aka Bongo Joe) hollers, whistles and grooves on his metal cans. I dare you not to groove along with his wild rants and street shuffle poetry. He is the Gene Krupa of the garbage cans.

--

"This is Bongo" Joe was the only record I stole from my campus radio station when I left. "Innocent Little Doggie" is the highlight here. It'll make you laff. Hell, if you're not careful, you might just learn something.

Did Beatniks Kill John F. Kennedy?

--

I remember Bongo Joe! He was all over the place in San Antonio when I was a little girl! When I was 4 or 5, I got to sit on his lap as he played during one of his performances.

--

oh. my. god... I haven't heard Bongo Joe in years! I remember him performing on the Galveston boardwalk when I was a little boy. I didn't even know he had a record. I still remember him beating away with broomsticks on those 55 gallon drums he had chained together while he whistled along... hahaha I remember that one of the sticks punched a hole in a drum lid... he paused, tuned that drum by tapping the stick and then away he went again... thank you SO much for this.

--

I am 59 and first heard Joe when I was 14 in 1968. KOME radio ... S.F.Bay Area radio. ALWAYS he has been in my head!!!!! :) R.I.P. Joe.

--

We were at the UTSA Texas cultures museum in San Antonio last spring and found the Bongo Joe exhibit. It included several photos and his bicycle with the home made drum kit. Now, here's the spooky part, while we were there this little elderly white lady comes up and starts visiting with us. Turns out she was George's girl friend back in the days that kind of thing was frowned on in Texas. She said when George died he was cremated and she still has his ashes at her home. That's my Bongo Joe story and it is the truth as far as I know.

Joe's list of dogs:

Bit-Paw, Bell-Miss, Sport, Raggs, Boxer, Pretty Boy, Joe Louis, Zooster, Ring (1 and 2), Browny (9 puppies), Blackie, Scrappy, Bamby, Shep, Junior (1 and 2), Little Whitey (1 and 2), Mommer Shepard, Babby Shep, Sandy, Daisy, Dutches, Gean-Maw, Shaggy. "We all wish you happy birthday/ yeah!"

Acknowledgments:

The author would like to thank the following persons for their contributions to this book:

Patrick B. Mullen, for sharing his interviews with Bongo Joe in 1967 and 1995 and for his enthusiastic support of this project; Cassie Patterson, Assistant Director, Center for Folklore Studies & Director of the Folklore Archives (Ohio State University), for facilitating the transfer of Pat Mullen's interviews with Bongo Joe from reel to reel to mp3; Nancy Grace, for helping with the publication of my article in the *Journal of Beat Studies*, and *JBS*'s Tony Trigilio for providing expert feedback on all things Beat and the Kennedy Assassination; Michael Mehl for his memories of working with Joe and for his clear-headed assessment of Joe's life and art; Kathleen Trenchard for her perseverance in preserving the memory of Bongo Joe; Jon Thompson for sending me a treasury of photos and images related to Bongo Joe, including his list of dogs; Sam Kendrick, for digging deep into his memories of covering Bongo Joe for the *San Antonio Express News*; George Nelson, for spending time recounting the making of his documentary on Bongo Joe; Giles McCrary, for his superb documentary on the Cellar and for sharing his contacts with me; Charlie Mitchell and Joe

Reese, Cellar musicians, for their insightful anecdotes about Joe and the club; Chris Strachwitz for taking a kind listen to the recovered tapes from Galveston, 1967; Jack Estes, for giving me one of the best interviews I have ever had the pleasure of hearing; Reynaldo Alvarado for his inspired cover art; Dashiell Johnson, for helping with the archival research at UT Austin; my children—Dashiell, Isabel, and Cactus—for sharing me with this book over the past five years and hopefully learning something about balancing one's life with one's passions; and my wife, Erika Garza-Johnson, for encouraging me when I needed it, telling me Joe's was a story that needed to be told.

Additional thanks: David Anshen, David Rice, Juan Ochoa, Pat O'Day, Chris Carmona, Chuck Taylor, Molly Ashley, Steven Davis, James Grauerholz.

My special thanks to David Wills, who took a chance on this book and its author.

This book is dedicated to Arvel Stricklin, Jr., who died in 2016. Arvel was the keeper of the Cellar flame and an endless help in answering all my questions related to the Cellar, Joe, and the Kennedy assassination. I could not have written the book without his help.

Notes on sources:

This book is written in a style that takes advantage of the techniques of creative non-fiction. When you write fiction, the aim is to make the story believable; when you write non-fiction, the aim is for readers to say at the end, "I can't believe that's true." But hopefully they do think it's true. I can say I believe everything in this book is true. I have tried to put a fact in every sentence. However, there are a few moments in the book where this is not strictly true. In dialogue between characters, for example, I sometimes imagine a facial response or intonation, albeit based on what that response or tone might plausibly be. I have on a few occasions invented dialogue for dramatic purposes, but only in the service of moving the narrative along, not for any substantive purpose. All of the rest of the dialogue comes from interviews, newspaper accounts, etc. To the best of my ability, and unless otherwise indicated in the text, I have strived to be as factual and as accurate as an encyclopedia entry. In other words, this is not a made-up story.

At the center of the book, however, is the story of Bongo Joe playing for the President. I believe this story to be true, although I have not been able to double-source it—the gold standard of research. The story is corroborated in part by Helen Glau, who said in Joe's obituary that he had played for the President at the Cellar nightclub the morning of his assassination. The latter is not true—playing at the nightclub—and easily checked by interviewing those who were at the nightclub that night the Secret Service showed up. In fact, the story would be well-known had Kennedy actually gone to the club. So if Joe played for the President, he must have played for him somewhere else, somewhere private, and close by the Cellar, where he was playing on a rotating set list that night. One other fact that corroborates and confuses the story a bit is that we know from newspaper accounts that Joe tried to play his drums the next morning on the stage built for Kennedy's speech in front of the Hotel Texas. Perhaps this was the "concert" he played for the President? But Joe was ordered off the stage well in advance of Kennedy's appearance that morning.

My source for the story of Joe playing for the President, alas, does not wished to be named, but the source was a longtime friend of Joe in San Antonio. I was able to contact a friend of the informant, retired in Texas, and speak through him to the source, who had suffered a stroke and was only able to communicate in whispers, making direct communication impossible. The friend took my questions from the phone to my source, and then relayed the responses. When I asked him about Joe playing for the President, the source's friend was gone from the phone a bit longer. When he returned, he told me the following: Yes, Joe had played for Kennedy that night. He was approached by the Secret Service, frisked, taken to a location near the nightclub, and performed for forty-five minutes. Specifically, the source relayed that Mrs. Kennedy was not present. After the performance, the President chatted with Joe and thanked him.

Joe wrote down his memories of this event on a piece of paper that has since been lost, but the source at one time saw it. The source's friend, who also knew Joe quite well, told this story with a tone of real surprise, and so I asked him, "Have you ever heard this story before?"

"Never," he told me.

"Did Joe make up stories?" I followed up.

He replied, "Not in my experience. He had no reason to do so."

After this conversation, they agreed to help with a more extensive interview at a later date; however, when I contacted the source's friend again, he declined: the informant was in very poor health, and thinking about Joe had triggered an emotional reaction that the source's friend believed was unhealthy. I didn't push it. In my experience, interviewing very old informants about sensitive information is just not humane.

So I have what I have, and was only able to corroborate it with circumstantial evidence, such as the fact that indeed Mrs. Kennedy would not have been there when Joe performed (she went to bed early in a separate hotel room); that Kennedy ordered a pot of coffee at 1 am (although he might have ordered that for the Secret Service guarding him); and that Joe had tried to play the stage in front of the Hotel Texas the next morning. I assumed, by the way, that Joe had been taken to a private room in the hotel that night to perform, as it was not possible Kennedy had been to the nightclub, and the Hotel Texas was only two blocks away. Arvel Stricklin, Jr. told me that it was indeed possible for Joe to leave the club for a period and return in time for his next performance. Would the staff at the Hotel Texas have revealed the story of Joe's performance that night? Not likely. It's remarkable how few people, including the members of the press, ever revealed information about Kennedy's doings "after hours," at least while he was alive.

Regarding the above, I'll admit it's frustrating my source is not definitive, but in my experience that's very in-line with so many stories surrounding the Kennedy assassination, which are often tantalizing but hard, finally, to nail down. At any rate, I hope to make the point in the book that what's more important than the assassination here is Joe's entire story, not just how his life intersected with Kennedy's death, although telling that story through the life of Bongo Joe certainly highlights new aspects of that tragedy.

The title of the book (not the subtitle) comes from an article I published in a refereed scholarly journal. The article dealt more generally with the "Beat" background of the Kennedy assassination and the Cellar nightclub, with a paragraph about "Bongo Joe." I kept the title knowing that both Kennedy assassination buffs and those interested in the life of men such as Joe might both like to take a look at the book.

There is actually new information about the Kennedy assassination here, and since assassination investigators are a precise and even fanatical lot, I'll summarize what's new and also what's a bit speculative on my part. My theory of the assassination is not my theory at all—I decided to use Arvel Stricklin, Jr.'s version of events, never before made public by him. That theory, in brief, is that Oswald was trying to shoot John Connally but there was a second shooter (or more than one) who simultaneously shot at Kennedy from the grassy knoll. Because of the set-up he saw at the Shrine Circus a few days before the assassination, and the reports of gunshots from the Coliseum that night, he believed the assassins were Italian snipers disguised as circus roustabouts. Stricklin also told me that in earshot of members of the service industry in Dallas and Fort Worth—waiters, waitresses, bus people, etc.—Oswald had been heard vilifying Connally. When I first contacted Stricklin, I originally was looking for stories about Bongo Joe, but he intimated he knew some things about the assassination that had never been publically voiced. He was quite hesitant to tell me his story—fearful of doing so—but eventually did. He even told this version of events to my students, via phone, during a course I taught on the Literature of the Kennedy Assassination in 2013. Stricklin, by the way, was unaware that anyone else (and it wasn't many) had ever suggested Oswald was trying to kill Connally, not Kennedy. I used his version of events because Arvel was working the Cellar that night and if there was a Beatnik theory of the assassination, it was Arvel's.

Is his version the truth? I have no idea, and in a way don't care, as all versions of the assassination are just stories and each version tells us something interesting about the times, the places, and the people involved. I was unable to corroborate Arvel's account of the platform up in the rafters of the Coliseum or the description of the clown car, but his account of the lights going out during the rehearsal was documented in the *Fort Worth Star-Telegram*. Also, after some effort, I was not able to find any account in the major newspapers of there being any gunshots coming from the Coliseum that night. To confirm that I would need to go through local police records. But I believe I'd find a report confirming his story: Arvel was quite definite about this incident, providing substantial details of what he had heard or read.

Other new information about the assassination is perhaps less dramatic but worth noting. The role of Little Lynn is important here. Arvel confirmed that she was in fact at the club the morning of the assassination, and when I told him Abraham Bolden's story of a badge being stolen that night at the Cellar, he immediately pointed the finger at her as the most likely suspect, being a suspiciously hard young woman and a well-known spy for Jack Ruby, who kept tabs on the success of local rival nightclubs. Dallas police records confirmed that Lynn was in fact also a police informant with a drug problem and links to prostitution and that she was spying on Kirkwood, too. No one, to my knowledge, has ever remarked on her story about Pat Kirkwood threatening her, told to the Warren Commission. It's quite dramatic, and the fact that there was no follow-up investigation is explained here for the first time: Kirkwood had done the Service a favor by lying about their drinking, and the Commission reciprocated by not pursuing what in any reasonable investigation would have been further questioning of Kirkwood's dealings. I gave Stricklin this passage of the Warren Commission Report to read and he told me Kirkwood was just trying to keep her quiet about his under-the-table business dealings, the fact that Kirkwood knew Jack Ruby (casually), and possibly the fact that Oswald had worked briefly at the San Antonio Cellar. Stricklin unequivocally told me that Kirkwood had nothing to do with the assassination—that this was ridiculous, Kirkwood actually liked Kennedy, Kirkwood had no connections to organized crime and was far too much of a radical individualist to be involved in a "plot." One other detail about Little Lynn is new—how she came into the possession of a pearl-handled pistol confiscated at Jack Ruby's pre-trial hearing.

How columnist Drew Pearson was tipped off about the Secret Service agents drinking at the Cellar is also revealed here for the first time, as is the presence of a rather large national news crew to cover a fairly routine set of campaign speeches by Kennedy: they were there primarily to cover the Wallenda's act.

No book on the assassination makes mention of Oswald briefly working as a dishwasher at the San Antonio location of the Cellar. This item popped up in a 1964 search of the *Express-News* featuring an interview with "Dubber." A later article featured Pat Kirkwood's similar version of the story. To be honest, I have no idea why Oswald was there, but I also have no reason to disbelieve Dubber and Kirkwood. Perhaps Oswald was laying low after trying to kill General

Did Beatniks Kill John F. Kennedy?

Walker. Perhaps he was looking for work in San Antonio. The timeline is a bit difficult to establish, but I was able to confirm that the Cellar was still in operation four days after Oswald was fired from his job in Fort Worth, and that it probably stayed open until mid-April. Oswald, unemployed, would have been able to make a trip to San Antonio, in other words, at some point after March 26th (the day he received his pink slip) or, if he continued to show up for work during the ten-day severance period following his termination, sometime in early-mid April. This coincides with Kirkwood and Dubber's story: Oswald, they say, worked there during the very last days of the San Antonio club's operation. Kirkwood, in a later interview in the 1980s, had apparently read up on Oswald's movements during those months and speculated that Oswald must have been returning from Mexico when he worked at the Cellar; but Oswald did not travel to Mexico until the summer of 1963, at the earliest, and the Cellar del Sur was shuttered by that point.

Two other new looks at the assassination: the long improvised history of the McKinley assassination by a reporter covering Kennedy's breakfast speech (available on YouTube as part of a much longer clip); and the conversation between the "beatnik" and the Chamber of Commerce volunteer. The latter is from an appendix to the Warren Commission report. Quite a few details in the book related to "beatniks" come from specialized searches of the entire Warren Commission report, available online. No one had previously searched the report through this specific historical and cultural lens.

Although I, of course, consulted the standard accounts of Kennedy's last days, and reproduced some agreed-upon facts, most of the information comes from primary sources such as newspapers, but also, for an example, an archived notebook kept by a reporter on the scene of the assassination, who records that the first suspect was a young black man. Because I was writing the story of a black man's life, I highlight that aspect of pre-civil rights society whenever possible. Therefore, I pay particular attention to material related to blacks in the service industry (the waiter who delivers Kennedy's morning coffee), and Jeb Byrne's memories of trying to integrate the Fort Worth events. And, of course, Abraham Bolden's dramatic story. This is not "new" information but it is information that has not been previously integrated as a whole into the story of Kennedy's last days. Bolden's story matched so well with Stricklin's story—independently—that I give it quite a bit of space.

My re-creation of the Cellar relies heavily on the dozens of newspaper stories Kirkwood's controversial club ginned up over the years, from the late 1950s through the early 1990s. Almost none of these stories figure into the mainstream magazine and otherwise historical accounts of the nightclub that have already been published. The reporters, most of whom drank there for free, had a good time writing these stories and I've re-created their zest and tone quite closely at times. My primary source of information, however, was Arvel Stricklin, Jr., to whom the book is dedicated (he died last year). Stricklin maintained a deep and detailed and illustrated website dedicated to the club, featuring many photographs given to him by Pat Kirkwood before Kirkwood died. Stricklin also interviewed many of the "Cellar Dwellers" on the site. This website has since disappeared, sadly, but I copied much of the texts before the site went dark as well as screen shots featuring photographs. I also interviewed Stricklin a dozen times over the phone and once in person in Fort Worth, where we visited the original sites of the nightclub and the Hotel Texas. Another major source of that section is original Cellar Dweller Jack Estes, whom I interviewed for two hours on the phone and followed up with email interviews. My long interview with Estes is featured in a book I co-edited titled *The Beatest State in the Union: Texas and the Beat Generation of Writers* (Lamar University Press, 2016). The McCrary film is also a source of information, but more importantly Giles put me in touch with several former Cellar musicians, who provide some of the details in this section, including their memories of "Cannibal Jones."

To tell the story of Bongo Joe, which has never been done in any comprehensive fashion, my sources as you can imagine were many and varied. I did deep searches of the San Antonio, Galveston, and Fort Worth newspapers, and much of my material is drawn from those sources. The largest cache of information is from the *San Antonio Express-News*, where Joe lived for the longest period of his life. I interviewed former Cellar Dwellers about their memories of Joe, people in Galveston who knew him, and of course several friends of Joe's in San Antonio, most of whom knew Joe during the later stages of his career there. A major source was the first folklorist to take Joe seriously as a performer and songwriter, Pat Mullen, and he directed me to the audio archives at Ohio State University, where he taught for many years. The helpful librarians there converted over four hours of audio tape from reel-to-reel to MP3, and they include a beachfront interview and recording of Joe's songs on the Seawall in 1967 and Pat's final interview with Joe, which also has an interview with Helen Glau. These tapes were invaluable and filled in many gaps in the story. They had not been heard by anyone other than Pat. I also corresponded with Chris Strachwitz and consulted his Arhoolie Records archives online. I use and quote from Larry Skoog's liner notes for Joe's album and his interview with Joe; I also took notes from Matt McCormick's extensive and fascinating "notes" for his 1958 anthology album "A Treasury of Field Recordings," a copy of which was available through the Fine Arts Library at The University of Texas at Austin. All song lyrics reproduced in the book come from Mullen's recordings and McCormick's "Treasury" and are in the public domain or used by permission.

In print books, of course, supplement the research, including books by Pat Mullen, Steven Davis (General Walker info and Dallas 1963 info), Abraham Bolden, Madeleine Duncan Brown

(LBJ's mistress), and many, many books on the Kennedy assassination, including James Reston, Jr.'s recent *The Accidental Victim*, which documents Oswald's attempt to kill John Connally.

Notes on the Text

1-10
longest sidewalk in the world ("Galveston Seawall"); six large cans he's bought ("Calypso's");"This Old World"(McCormick); currently playing a nearby drive-in ("Calypso"); born in Florida in 1923/other biographical details, Joe's life in Galveston in 1950's (Wortham; Mullen); In Detroit in 1941 (AI); Davis also meets Frank Sinatra/ Sinatra himself introduces the Mastin Trio (Kaplan 251-253); In later years (AI); both Joe and Sammy entertain troops as part of the Entertainment Corps (Mullen 1995); "My talent was the weapon" (Cook); A picture (Mullen 1995); At the end of the war in 1946 (Mullen 1995); Houston has one of the largest population of blacks (Wood 28); "the best state I ever been in" (Skoog); "Just trying to get a job as a drummer"(McCormick); Texas Gulfliner, depot description (Bogren); he lives behind Menard Park (AI2). Frank Sinatra plays there in 1950 (Smith, William Michael); eats chili and beans at the Speedway Café (Cherry); can't get a room in the Vegas hotels (Cook); Joe plays conga ("Big"); Billy Bentley (Dansby).

11-20:
cast of big city characters (McCormick); summer of 1958, Pat Kirkwood (AS); wild and wooly frontier town (much of the description of Fort Worth's frontier past comes from McCrary, particularly Bob Schieffer's portrait of his hometown's rowdy past); Pat Jr. is born at the 2222 (Cochran, "Party's"); "younger, taller wilder version of

Pappy" ("Offbeat"); Kirkwood has a career as a stock-car driver (AS); drives a Cadillac; races against a Lincoln Sapri and Chrysler 300 (Freeport); Johnny Carroll (AS; CW; "Johnny"); It's Kirkwood's car/Kirkwood wins a small property (AS); George Carlin (Brooks, "Ex-Fort"); "Kerouac sold" (Burroughs 180); San Francisco beatnik clubs (Morgan); Café Bizarre (Van Ronk 54-55); on September 24, 1959 (CH); a true walk-down, subterranean club/other descriptions of the Cellar (AS; JE).

21-30

Folk musician Jack Estes (JE); Johnny Carroll takes over (AS); "a combination of ancient fertility rituals" (Brooks "Bounced"); E. Clive Whitlock (Brooks "Whatever"); playing only the black keys (AS); if a Negro wants in the club badly/have their own small dressing room (AS); it's too much fun, dangerously fun (AS; JE); "V-rroom!" (AS, CM); Fort Worth Stock Show Parade (JR); "Communists, eggheads, and beatniks" ("Herbert"); slate of "Beatnik" candidates"/National Beatnik Week ("Politics"); series of police raids (Cochran "Lost"; "Beatniks"); Kirkwood himself has summoned the cops (AS); Melba Hotel burns down (Bowles); 8 feet high and 3 feet of smoke (AS); place is "neater" and "cleaner" (Brooks "New"); San Antonio Cellar (Brooks "Cellar"); performance by Little Lynn (Kindrick "Oswald"); make the club a hit (AS); "Animal Jones" (Kindrick "Hemisfair's"); phony murder (Thompson); give her a pearl- handled pistol (Kindrick "Oswald"); Jack Ruby ("Cellar"); Cellar Del Sur doesn't last long ("Beatnik"); Lee Harvey Oswald (Kindrick "Oswald"); Oswald on discharge and Connally (de Mohrenschildt 84; 145; 148); Oswald's admiration of Kennedy (de Mohrenschildt 89; 132-133; 146); Oswald's views on discrimination (de Mohrenschildt 119-120; 127; 133; 184; 198); de Mohrenschildt asks Oswald about shooting General Walker (de Mohrenschildt 200); "this is the hunter of fascists" (de Mohrenschildt 256).

31-40

General Walker (Minutaglio and Davis); Abraham Bolden (Bolden, Echo; "First"); daytime rehearsal of the Shrine Circus (AS; Brooks "All"); Karl Wallenda (Brooks "All") NBC news crew (Brooks "All"); Happy Keller (Brooks "All"); gunshots (AS); advance team, Fort Worth (Byrne); Negro agent denied room at Hotel Texas (Sanders); Kennedy lands/"Goldwater in 1864"; echo chamber (Johnson, "JFK"); room 850 (Wysatta); separate bedrooms/ French works (Meslay); own gathering (Brown 167); orders a pot of coffee (Bishop); drinking on the plane (Bolden).

41-50

invited to a "party" (Brown 166); Bob Schieffer and Phil Record (Schieffer, p. 3 ff); Jack Ruby's strippers (including Little Lynn) there as well (AS; Anderson); makes a phone call (AS); details Cellar party Nov. 22, 1963 (AS; McCrary; Anderson); He has an affair (see, for example, Hersh, Talbot); "typical beatnik" (Warren); naked lunch (Jacobs 91); Jacques Lowe/*Reader's Digest* (Amburn 317); lunched with Jackie (Amburn 358); "Brooks Brothers Beatnik" (Hilty 192); too free-thinking (Leight); Joe's Story/writes down his memories/never been known to make up stories (AI); misplaces his badge (Bolden 103-104); George Jackson (Bishop 15-18); shot me (Byrne); They both carry pistols (AS); Bongo Joe is in the crowd (Mariani); footage of the crowd ("JFK's); details of morning speech (Hamilton); $100,000 dollars (Lasky 144); no negro citizens (Byrne); McKinley assassination ("November"); arrive in the Ballroom ("November"—full speech; discussion of McKinley assassination, 5:36 forward)

51-60:

Donald C. Bubar (Bubar); Charlie Whomper (AS); "Let's Barry the President" (Mueller); mouthing off (AS); target is Texas Governor John Connally (AS; Reston); "sacred" private property rights (Wilkinson); Connally hears

("John"); disguised as Shrine Circus roustabouts (AS); first suspect (" A Reporter's"); Joe Smith ("Testimony of Joe"); Pat Kirkwood hears ("Cellar"; AS); business as usual (AS); gonna get lynched (JE); lost their badge (Bolden; "First"); Bud Shrake (BS); wires Carousel dancer ("Testimony of Mrs."); go back to Dallas ("Cellar"; AS); funeral of Abraham Lincoln (Lubin; Piereson); interrogates Kirkwood and Cellar manager Dick Mackie ("Letter"; "Cellar"); Kirkwood and Mackie have their story straight/ make their case more than plain ("You"; interview with Jim Hill in McCrary 49:45 ff); find the little pistol ("Cellar"; "December"); "Oh my God they are after me"/threatened by Pat Kirkwood ("Testimony Of Mrs."); an informant ("Transcript"); number one suspect (AS); knows too much/ you never make it inside ("Transcript"); Right had long warned (Piereson 92 ff); fitting the stereotype of the Beatnik communist (Courtwright); two other beatnik looking boys ("The Lopez"); beatnik style (Warren Commission Exhibit 2909); looked like a typical beatnik ("City"); was not a Beatnik (Warren Commission Exhibit 2460);

61-70

agent drops a dime (Bolden; "First"); film is put off/ Southern bases the character/too pinko for The Duke/real good time in Dallas (Southern 72 ff); Cellar "The Attic" (Brooks "Oliver"); post-Beatles British invasion rock and roll club/freehands "Rock" (AS; CM; JR); completely disassembled (AS); Beachcomber Club ("Isle"); defined in three letters (Wolfe); What I like about the jungle is (Mullen, *Man*); Read all about it (Mullen, "Original"); "How about a little 'Wipe Out'?" (Mullen, "Original"); Joe loses his stage (Skoog); razing the historical site (Keller; Palmer); money flowed like water (Kindrick "Big"); English Bulldog (Kindrick "Bongo"); understanding between peoples (Oefinger); I've got a dollar ("Fair"); "Are you Mexican or American?" ("Hemisfair is"); protestors (McCrory); memorial for Dr. King (Denman); "He's just plain good" (Kindrick "George"); A beat like I've never heard/Just three blocks/If your Daddy ("HemisFair").

71-80;
Strachwitz bio (Flemons); "Master what?"/ "Talk, talk, Joe." (Mullen, "Original"); an album of vitality (*Rolling Stone*); interview with Joe (Skoog); liner notes (Skoog, Lawrence C.); "The Magic Negro" (suggested by MM); Sun Ra (Campbell); some kind of mystical protection (MM); we've got to help him (Stinson); I'm not going (Mullen, "Original" 1995); home of Marshall Steves (Lander); Ford unashamedly scavenges (Dillon 117-118); Muhammed Ali (Crouse); New Orleans Jazz and Heritage Festival/ copy of his contract (Kindrick, "Offbeat" Apr 27, 1971); Joe and Dizzy (Smith, Michael P., p. 32 [picture of Joe and Gillespie]).

81-90
birthday party for Joe (Kindrick "Offbeat"); Joe Ely (McCrary, 108:58 ff; McCrary liner notes "Joe Ely"); black TCU students are denied admission (Elston "Whatever"); deer hunting season ("City Receives"); Kirkwood will admit who he wants to ("Cellar Owner"); August 19, 1972, the Cellar closes (Kidd); Paredes mentors (Nadler 44); Joe performs for his second President ("Texans"); screens it on the national TV ("The Zapruder"); a high probability/ no agent violated any Secret Service Rule ("The Lopez Report"); "he would have joined the group of love-children" (de Mohrenschildt 97); typical evening in the 1970's (King); John Phillip Santos "City of Dreams"; Joe witnesses a man wield a knife/Joe pulls out his .45 ("Bongo Joe"); the police seem to keep their distance from Joe (KT); survivors of the Alamo siege were executed ("La Antorcha"); "Bongo Joe You Are Forever" (photo) http://ww3.hdnux.com/phot os/35/30/40/7702550/5/920x920.jpg; spot Joe performing (AS); reporter Jack Anderson hosts (Anderson); the stage at the Tenth and Main location (AS); "Double or Nothing"

(Cochran"Deuces").

91-end
"Almost Live from the Liberty Bar" (Conroy; MM); premature obituary (Teutsch); The last interview (Mullen Original); Joe dies (Crouse); concentrate on preserving the legacy of "high-brow" (AI 3); Kathleen Trenchard (KT); Antonio's Institute of Texan Cultures (Schwartz; Teutsch); a thousand coffee shops (Burroughs 180); 50th anniversary of the Kennedy Assassination (Carlisle); *Texas Monthly* (Graham); Billy Ray Cyrus ("Billy"); Cellar documentary film (Lin); "Rufus Jones for President" ("Rufus"); Joe's Kennedy pipe photographed after his death as part of altar created by Kathleen Trenchard, which also included a photo of Joe smoking the pipe, circa late 1960's, in his black Cellar turtleneck shirt; list of dogs (courtesy of Jon Thompson).

Informants:
Arvel Stricklin, Jr. (AS); Jack Estes (JE); Kathleen Trenchard (KT); Sam Kendrick (SK); Charlie Mitchell (CM); Joe Reese (JR); Michael Mehl (MM); George Nelson (GN); Ben Shrake (BS); Anonymous Informant (see "Afterword") (AI); Anonymous Informant 2 (AI2— acquaintance of Joe's in Galveston, 1960's); AI 3 (friend of Joe's in San Antonio, early 1990's). I interviewed Stricklin, a primary source, numerous times by email, phone, and in-person in Fort Worth, between 2010 and 2015. Articles cited as "on line" are accessible by their titles through a Google search. Other links provided.

Works Cited
Amburn, Ellis. *Subterranean Kerouac*. New York: St
    Martin's Press, 1998.

"An album of vitality." *Rolling Stone*, Sept. 20, 1969, p.36.

Anderson, Jack. "American Expose: Who Murdered John F. Kennedy?" https://www.youtube.com/watch?v=oDbodTKnTjc. 55:50 forward.

"A Reporter's Notes." https://www.tsl.texas.gov/sites/default/files/public/tslac/landing/documents/jfk-upi_feed-2.pdf. UPI A59N.

"Beatnik Cellar Going Off Limits." *San Antonio Express-News*, Feb. 10, 1963 p. 9.

"Beatniks Return to Cellar After Battle With Cops." *Galveston Daily News*, Aug 23, 1961, p. 2. Reprinted from *Fort Worth Star Telegram*.

"Big Crowd Sees Blue Room Show." *Galveston Daily News*, June 13, 1957, p. 12.

"Billy Ray Cyrus: Super-Awkward Tribute to JFK" (TMZ) https://www.youtube.com/watch?v=mwz6hY4hazo

Bishop, Jim. *The Day Kennedy Was Shot*. New York: Funk & Wagnalls, 1968.

Bogren, Scott. "A Once and Future Great Train Station" (online).

Bolden, Abraham. *The Echo From Dealey Plaza*. New York: Crown, 2008.

"Bongo Joe Involved in Shooting." *Galveston Daily News* April 12, 1983, p. 2.

Bowles, Pete. "Beatnik Night Spot Destroyed by Fire." *Fort Worth Star-Telegram*, Feb. 7, 1962, Sect. 2, p. 7.

Brooks, Elston. "All Eyes on Highwire as Wallendas Rehearse." *Fort Worth Star-Telegram*, Nov 20, 1963, Sect. 2, p. 5.

----- "Bounced Dog." *Fort Worth Star-Telegram*, Mar 15, 1961, p 13.

-----"Cellar del Sur Opens in Alamo City." *Fort Worth Star-Telegram*, Dec. 12, 1962, Sect. 2, p. 7.

-----"Ex-Fort Worth Pair Hit Comedy Big-Time." *Fort Worth Star-Telegram*, Aug. 7, 1961, section 1, p. 7.

-----"New Cellar Cleaner and Neater." *Fort Worth Star-Telegram*, Mar 5, 1962, Sect. 1, p. 4.

-----"Oliver Brightens Holidays." *Fort Worth Star-Telegram*, Dec. 31, 1964, sect. 1, p. 6.
-----"Whatever Happened to Pat Kirkwood?" *Fort Worth Star-Telegram*. Oct. 15, 1978, p. F-1.
Brown, Madeleine Duncan. *Texas in the Morning: The Love Story of Madeleine Brown and President Lyndon Baines Johnson*. Conservatory Press, 1997.
Bubar, Donald C. Interview, *Warren Commission Report*, Volume 18, p. 691. Commission Exhibit 1020.
Burroughs, William S. "Remembering Jack Kerouac," in *The Adding Machine: Selected Essays*, New York: Seaver Books, 1986.
Byrne, Jeb "The Hours Before Dallas." On line.
"Calyspso Joe." *Galveston Daily News*, Aug 23, 1957, p.5.
"Calypso's Drummin' Again on Beachfront." *Galveston Daily News*, Aug 22, 1957, p.1.
Campbell, Robert L. et. al., *From Sonny Blount to Sun Ra: The Chicago Years*. http://campber.people.clemson.edu/sunra.html. Sun Ra story reprinted from *Chicago Defender*, July 6, 1957, p. 30.
Carlisle, Candace. "JFK 50th: Limited tickets for the Dealey Plaza memorial." *Dallas Business Journal*, June 20, 2013. Online.
"Cellar Case Brings Fines for Owner." *Fort Worth Star-Telegram*, Dec. 8, 1971, p. 1.
"Cellar Owner Holds to Policy." *Fort Worth Star-Telegram*, Mar 18, 1971, p. 3-C.
"Cellar Owner Recalls Long FBI Quizzing." *Fort Worth Star-Telegram*, Sept. 28, 1964, Sect. 2, p. 4.
Cherry, Bill. "A Story You Don't Know About Frank Sinatra." http://activerain.com/blogsview/272968/a-story-you-don-t-know-about-frank-sinatra-----by-dallas-realtor-bill-cherry
City of New Orleans Assistant DA Andrew Sciambra memo regarding his interview with Perry Raymond Russo at the Mercy Hospital on February 27, 1967. http://mcadams.posc.mu.edu/russo3.txt

"City Receives Indefinite Delay in Cellar Case." *Fort Worth Star-Telegram*, Oct. 27, 1971, p. 16-A.

Cochran, Mike. "Deuces Wild." *Dallas Morning News*, May 7, 1991, A-1; A-10.

-----"Lost Sheep Losing Way Without Den." *Denton Record-Chronicle*, August, 20 1961. Reprinted from *Fort Worth Star-Telegram.*

-----"Party's Almost Over for State's Wicked Thunder Road." *Del Rio News-Herald*, March 20, 1988, p. 7, B. Reprinted from *Fort Worth Star-Telegram.*

Conroy, Ed. "Offbeat Show Makes It into Mainstream." *San Antonio Current*, July 25-August 2 1991. http://michaelmehl.com/1991-michael-mehl-san-antonio-current-almost-live-from-the-liberty-bar-on-klrn-tv/

Cook, Everett. "Breaking racial barriers." *The Desert Sun,* Oct 18, 2015. http://www.desertsun.com/story/life/entertainment/2015/10/18/rat-pack-sammy-davis-jr/74069042/

Courtwright, Chris. "Oswald in Aliceland? A Tale of Two Days; A Tale of Two Oswalds." Presented to JFK Lancer's November in Dallas Conference on November 21, 1997. http://jfklancer.com/Page1.html

Crouse, Jacque and Beal, Jim. "Downtown Fixture Bongo Joe Dies." *San Antonio Express-News*, Dec 21, 1999. p 1.

Dansby, Andrew. "Profile: Bill Bentley." *Houston Chronicle*, May, 28, 2013. On line.

"December 23, 1963 – "Karen 'Little Lynn' Bennett arrested at Jack Ruby's trial for carrying a gun." https://www.youtube.com/watch?v=nC3L0cUeF5s

De Mohrenschildt, George. "I Am a Patsy! I Am a Patsy!" Appendix, *Staff Report of Select Committee on Assassinations*, 1979.

Denman, Bob. "Dr. King Mourned in S. A." *San Antonio Express-News*, April 8, 1968, p. 1.

Dillon, David. *The Architecture of O'Neil Ford: Celebrating Place*. Austin: University of Texas

Press, 1999. pp. 117-118

"Fair Fans Walk, Talk and Gawk as Gates Open." *San Antonio Express-News*, April 8, 1968, p. 22-H.

"First Black Secret Service Agent, Abraham Bolden, Speaks Out on Being Framed & JFK Assassination." https://www.youtube.com/watch?v=1xEf8gm-r8M

Flemons, Don. "It's Got Ahold of Me." *Oxford American Magazine*, Winter 2014.

http://www.oxfordamerican.org/magazine/item/402-it-s-got-ahold-of-me

Freeport Facts May 19, 1955, p. 2.

"Galveston Seawall." *Wikipedia*.

Glau, Helen. "More on Bongo Joe" (letter to the Editor*)*. *San Antonio Express-News*, Aug 22, 1976, 16-A.

Graham, Don. "The Class of '63.*"* *Texas Monthly*, Nov 2013. http://www.texasmonthly.com/articles/the-class-of-63/

Hamilton, Caroline. "Early Birds Got Best Views, But Everybody Grew Taller." *Fort Worth Press*, Nov 22, 1963.

Heinkel-Wolff, Peggy. "Shelton Detailed History." Denton Record-Chronicle.com (DRC.com), November 2013.

"Hemisfair '68" https://tshaonline.org/handbook/online/articles/lkh01

"Hemisfair is for the Rich Only." *San Antonio Express-News*, Apr 7, 1968, 24-H.

"Herbert Hoover 1960 Republican Convention" https://www.youtube.com/watch?v=oCfBAM0J7YI

Hersh, Seymour. *The Dark Side of Camelot*. New York: Little Brown & Co, 1997.

Hilty, James W. *Robert Kennedy: Brother Protector*. Temple University Press, 2000.

"Isle Beachcomber to Open Today." *Galveston News-Tribune*, June 1964, 6-A.

Jacobs, George and Stadiem, William. "Sinatra and the Dark Side of Camelot." *Playboy*, June 2003, p. 91 ff.

"JFK's 'Parking Lot' Speech." https://www.youtube.com/

watch?v=FYHchIwWC2Y.

"John Connally Debunked JFK 'Single-Bullet Theory.' " Preview of Jerome R. Corsi's *Who Really Killed Kennedy? Fifty Years Later* (2013). Includes extensive testimony by John Connally. On line.

Johnson, Ed. "JFK Lands Amid Roar of Cheers." *Fort Worth Star-Telegram*, Nov. 22, 1963, p. 1.

Johnson, Rob, "Did Beatniks Kill John F. Kennedy?" *Journal of the Beat Studies Association*, Volume 2 (2013).

----- *The Beatest State in the Union: Texas and the Beat Generation of Writers*, ed. Beaumont: Lamar University Press, 2016.

Kaplan, James. *Frank: the Voice*. New York: Random House, 2011.

Keller, Carol A. "HemisFair '68 and the Cultural Matrix of San Antonio," p. 20 ff.

https://www.google.com/url?sa=t&rct=j&q=&esrc=s&source=web&cd=3&ved=0ahUKEwi6j9bbp7HSAhUK22MKHZxgBREQFggkMAI&url=http%3A%2F%2Fibrarian.net%2Fnavon%2Fpaper%2FHemisFair__68_and_the_Cultural_Matrix_of_San_Anto.pdf%3Fpaperid%3D15406095&usg=AFQjCNG05L5Px6_kHy4Zcp-9c39nrTwRDA&bvm=bv.148073327,d.cGc

Kidd, Tim. "Cellar Bows Out With No Fanfare." *Fort Worth Star-Telegram*, Aug 19, 1972, p. 9-C.

Kindrick, Sam. "Big Daddy of All Fiestas is a Gusher." *San Antonio Express-News*, Apr 7, 1968, p. 1-X.

-----"Bongo Joe Really Can Make a Piano Talk." *San Antonio Express-News*, Sept 14, 1970, p. 11.

-----"George Coleman is Plenty Good." *San Antonio Express-News*, May 29, 1968, C-1.

-----"Hemisfair Over But Bongo Joe Remains." *San Antonio Express-News*, Oct 14, 1968, p. 11.

----- "Offbeat." *San Antonio Express-News*, Apr 27, 1971, p 7-B.

----- "Offbeat." *San Antonio Expres-News*, Dec 1, 1973, p 7-E.

King, Ben, Jr. "Bongo Joe Is." *San Antonio Express-News Sunday Magazine*, Dec 26, 1976, p. 3.

"La Antorcha de la Amistad." https://en.wikipedia.org/wiki/La_Antorcha_de_la_Amistad.

Lander, Larry. *San Antonio Hometown Tour: A Travel Journal*. http://www.ricedesignalliance.org/2012/san-antonio-hometown-tour-a-travel-journal/

Lasky, Victor. *It Didn't Start With Watergate*. New York: E P Dutton, 1977.

Leight, Michele. "Jacqueline Kennedy: The White House Years." http://www.thecityreview.com/jackieo.htmly

Letter from the Secret Service to the Commission, pp. 666-667. Warren Commission, Volume XVIII: CE 1019.

Lin, Kristian. "Cellar Dwellers: A Local Filmmaker Documents a Historic Fort Worth Music Club." *Fort Worth Weekly*, May 8, 2013.

Lubin, David M. *Shooting Kennedy: JFK and the Culture of Images*. Berkeley: University of California Press, 2003. Excerpt: http://www.businessinsider.com/jfk-funeral-arrangement-2013-11#ixzz3XOakhBsD

Mariani, Anthony. "Cellar Star Bongo Joe Remembered." *Fort Worth Weekly*, Feb. 15, 2010. On line.

McCormick, Mack McCormick. *A Treasury of Field Recordings*, Volume 2, 77 Records (77LA12/3), 1960. Includes liner notes.

McCrary, Giles. *You Must Be Weird Or You Wouldn't Be Here* (2013). Documentary film, including biographical liner notes on Cellar regulars, workers, and performers. www.youmustbeweird.com

McCrory, James. "Everyone at the Fair—Pickets, Too." *San Antonio Express-News*, Apr 7, 1968, p. 24-H.

Meslay, Olivier, et. al. *Hotel Texas: An Art Exhibition for the President and Mrs. John F. Kennedy*. New Haven: Yale University Press, 2013.

Minutaglio, Bill, and Davis, Steven L. *Dallas 1963*.

Twelve Publishers, 1963.

Morgan, Bill. *The Beat Generation in San Francisco: A Literary Tour*. San Francisco: City Lights Books, 2003.

Mueller, Tracy. "Why JFK Died in Dallas." Excerpt from *Dallas 1963*, by Bill Minutaglio and Steven L. Davis. On line.

Mullen, Patrick B. *The Man Who Adores the Negro*. University of Illinois Press, 2008

----- Original reel-to-reel recording of an interview with George "Bongo Joe" Coleman conducted by Pat Mullen April 8, 1967, Galveston Seawall; 1995 interview, Audie Murphy Hospital, San Antonio, Texas. MP3 of four tape reels provided to author courtesy of Cassie Patterson, Assistant Director, Center for Folklore Studies & Director of the Folklore Archives, Ohio State University.

Nadler, Maggie. "The Blues Brothers: Two Graduates Chronicle Texas' Roots Music," *The Alcalde* May-Jun 1994, p. 44.

"November 22, 1963 - President John F. Kennedy's Remarks at the Fort Worth Chamber of Commerce" (5:36 ff) https://www.youtube.com/watch?v=w18UnPjkrwc

Oefinger, Myrtle. "First Lady Enthusiastic in Her Dedication Roles," *San Antonio Express-News*, Apr 7, 1968, p. 25-H.

"Offbeat." *Kerrville Times*, May 6, 1991, p. 2.

Palmer, Timothy James. "HemisFair '68: The Confluence of Politics in San Antonio." MA Thesis, UT Austin, 1990.

Pearson, Drew. "Merry-Go-Round." Dec. 2, 1963. Included in "The Secret Service, FBI, and Dallas Police." Warren Commission Exhibit 1020, p. 677.

Piereson, James. *Camelot and the Cultural Revolution: How the Assassination of JFK Shattered American Liberalism*. New York: Encounter Books, 2007.

"Politics: Beat in the Hip of Texas." *Life*, Mar 6, 1960, p. 48.

Rand, Ayn. "JFK—High Class Beatnik?" *Human Events*, Sept 1, 1960. On line.

Reston, James. *The Accidental Victim: JFK, Lee Harvey Oswald, and The Real Target in Dallas*. Zola Books, 2013.

"Rufus Jones for President." https://www.youtube.com/watch?v=2nV_MmcQIGPc

Sanders, Bob Ray. "Three Great Exhibits Recount JFK's Visit to Fort Worth 50 Years Ago," November 2013. http://www.star-telegram.com/news/special-reports/jfk/article3836220.html

Santos, John Phillip. "City of Dreams," *Texas Monthly*, June 2010. http://www.texasmonthly.com/articles/city-of-dreams/

Schieffer, Bob. *This Just In: What I Couldn't Tell You on TV*. New York: Putnam, 2003.

Schwartz, Eileen. "A Great Weekend in San Antonio." *Texas Monthly*, Nov 2002. On line.

Skoog, Larry, and Strachwitz, Chris. "Bongo Joe (George Coleman) Interview." 1968. http://arhoolie.org/bongo-joe-george-coleman-interview/

Skoog, Lawrence C. "Bongo Joe" George Coleman. Arhoolie Records 1040, 1968, liner notes.

Smith, Michael P. *New Orleans Jazz Fest: A Pictorial History*. Gretna, LA: Pelican Publishing Company, 1991.

Smith, William Michael. "When Frank Sinatra Played Juarez . . . And Galveston." *Houston Press*, Oct. 21, 2010. On line.

Southern, Terry. "Strangelove Outtake: Notes from the War Room." In Southern, Nile, ed., *Now Dig This: The Unspeakable Writings of Terry Southern, 1950-1995*. Grove Press, 2002.

Stinson, Roddy. "A Switch Massage, A Horse, Bongo Joe—And Thou." *San Antonio Express-News*, Dec

17, 1976, 3-A.

Talbot, David. *Brothers: The Hidden History of the Kennedy Years*. Free Press, 2007.

Teutsch III, Tucker. "Ofrenda's and Offerings." *San Antonio Current*, Oct 31, 2002. https://www.sacurrent.com/sanantonio/ofrendas-and-offerings/Content?oid=2266583

"Testimony of Joe Marshall Smith." Warren Commission Hearings and Exhibits, volume VII, p. 535, as cited in the History Matters Archive, http://www.history-matters.com/archive/jfk..._Vol7_0272a.htm

ITC staffer Willie Mendez

"Testimony of Mrs. Bruce Carlin." http://mcadams.posc.mu.edu/russ/testimony/carlin_k2.htm.

"Texans Welcome Impressive Sight." *Pampa News*, April 27, 1976, p. 8.

"The Lopez Report": *HSCA Report on the Kennedy Assassination*, Appendix 13, p. 206.

"The Zapruder Film is Showed on Good Night America" (March 6, 1975). https://www.youtube.com/watch?v=nxCH1yhGG3Q

Thompson, Paul. "Pat Kirkwood and the Cellar." *San Antonio Express-News*, Jan 6, 1963, p. 1.

"Transcript of the interrogation of Karen Lynn Bennet, aka Little Lynn, a stripper at Jack Ruby's Carousel Club." Dallas Police Department. Date unknown (circa Feb. 1964). https://texashistory.unt.edu/ark:/67531/metapth190037/

Van Ronk, Dave. *The Mayor of McDougal Street: A Memoir by Dave Van Ronk*. De Capo Press, 2013.

Warren Commission Exhibit 1025.

Warren Commission Exhibit 2460.

Warren Commission Exhibit 2909.

Wilkinson, Gordon. "Civil Rights Demonstration in Austin (1963)." Texas Archive of the Moving Image. On line.

Wolfe, Tom. *The Electric Kool Aid Acid Test*. New York:

Farrar, Straus, and Giroux, 1968.
Wood, Roger. *Down in Houston.* Austin: University of Texas Press, 2003.
Wortham, Fred. "Calypso Drums Fade From Wail to Jail." *Galveston Daily News*, Aug 21, 1957, p.1.
Wysatta, Jean. "Suite 850 . . . It'll Be Famous." *Fort Worth Press*, November 17, 1963.

www.ingramcontent.com/pod-product-compliance
Lightning Source LLC
Chambersburg PA
CBHW070628300426
44113CB00010B/1697